THE TESTAMENT OF LIGHT

HE THAT BELEEVES IN THE LIGHT HATH THE
WITNESS WITHIN HIMSELF

THE
TESTAMENT
OF
LIGHT

AN ANTHOLOGY OF
SPIRITUAL WISDOM
DRAWN FROM MANY
AGES AND LITERATURES

BY GERALD BULLETT

WINGS BOOKS
NEW YORK • AVENEL, NEW JERSEY

This 1994 edition is published by Wings Books,
distributed by Random House Value Publishing, Inc.,
40 Engelhard Avenue, Avenel, New Jersey 07001,
by arrangement with Alfred A. Knopf, Inc.

Random House
New York • Toronto • London • Sydney • Auckland

Printed and bound in the United States of America

Library of Congress Cataloging-in-Publication Data
The testament of light : an anthology / made and
edited by Gerald Bullett.
p.   cm.
Originally published: New York: Knopf, 1932.
Includes index.
ISBN 0-517-11986-2
I. Bullett, Gerald William, 1894-1958.
PN6071 R4T47   1994
082—dc20
[082]   94-30527
                                      CIP
8 7 6 5 4 3 2 1

PREFACE

THIS IS AN ANTHOLOGY OF
the religious spirit, a collection of utterances testifying
to the 'divinity' in man, the inwardness of authority,
the redemptive power of that love (within us, not elsewhere) 'whose service is perfect freedom'. It suggests
a philosophy of life without intending either to establish a theological system or to beg the question of theism itself. In a book whose whole aim is to exalt the
spirit and neglect the letter, literalism will hardly be
looked for: it has been enough for my purpose that
these chosen authors, in these particular instances,
have wielded (in Boehme's phrase) 'the hammer that
can strike my bell'; and the conviction that I am not
singular in this responsiveness prompts me (beyond
my first intention) to make my choice public. I have
chosen sparingly from the literature of mysticism and
mystical philosophy, and always in search rather of
spiritual than intellectual enlightenment. However real
may be the experience that inspires them, such radiant
theorizings are inevitably something in the nature of
mythology. The scope of literal statement is narrow indeed; all that is vital in our experience carries us far
beyond it. We ask of a myth, not that it shall be true

in fact, but that it shall dramatize, in a poetic fiction, our otherwise indefinable apprehensions and aspirations. The God Idea, in its innumerable forms, figures forth the fears, hopes, and desires of man, as well as his guesses at the nature of things. The god of the savage is a savage; the god of the moral pedant is a moral pedant; of the mathematician, a mathematician; of the poet, a poet. By their gods ye shall know them. Nevertheless, we are divided less by our differences of formal belief, our theism and our atheism, than by something at once more vital and less easy of definition; something of which the nature will be immediately apparent to responsive readers of this TESTA-MENT OF LIGHT, especially to those who will consent to read its contents in the order given, regarding it as a single continuing discourse lightened (but not broken) by lyrical interludes. I do not question that many other passages tending to the same purpose might have been found by a compiler more widely acquainted than I am with the literature of my theme; and suggestions for the enrichment of the anthology will be gratefully considered, and acted upon (so far as may be) in subsequent editions. But, even so, what I offer here is the result of no little sifting; much has been first chosen and then rejected; and much else has been deliberately avoided. I have refrained, for example, after due consideration, not only from such writers and sources as Plotinus, Proclus, Pascal, Saint Augustine, Thomas à Kempis, and the Bhagavadgita, but from many of our English poets and prose writers who must have found a place in any anthology of which literary excellence was the sole or chief criterion.

My warmest thanks are due to those authors, publishers, and copyright-owners generally, who have kindly permitted me to include copyright matter: Lascelles Abercrombie, Dodd, Mead and Company (for 46), and Martin Secker Ltd (for 107); Martin Armstrong; H. G. Wells; George Russell (A E) and The Macmillan Company; Macmillan's again, for use of Davies and Vaughan's translation of Plato's *Republic*; W. J. Turner and Wishart and Co; Siegfried Sassoon and Harper and Brothers; Richard Church and J. M. Dent and Sons Ltd; Frank Kendon; Logan Pearsall Smith and Doubleday, Doran and Company; George Santayana and Charles Scribner's Sons; Harry Roberts and the Editor of *The New Statesman and Nation;* P. J. and A. E. Dobell and Charles Scribner's Sons (for Traherne's *Centuries of Meditations*); E. P. Dutton and Company (for Richard Jefferies); the Clarendon Press (for Robert Bridges); Alfred A. Knopf Inc. (for Homer P. Earle's translation of Unamuno); Lionel Giles and E. P. Dutton and Company (for the translation of *Confucius*); Walter Gorn Old and Rider and Co (for the translation of *Lao-Tze*); the Egypt Exploration Fund (for *The New Sayings of Jesus*). For criticism, and help of various kinds, I am specially grateful to my friends Ruth Niven, Marie Brahms, Francis and Vera Meynell, E. J. D. Radclyffe, E. M. W. Tillyard, and, not least, my wife. Finally, of any whose claims have been inadvertently overlooked, or whose kindness remains unacknowledged, I ask forgiveness.

May 1932   G. B.

DILIGE ET QVOD VIS FAC
SIVE FACEAS DILECTIONE FACEAS
RADIX SIT INTVS DILECTIONIS
NON POTEST DE ISTA RADICE
NISI BONVM EXISTERE

THE
TESTAMENT
OF
LIGHT

1

YOU ARE AS PRONE TO LOVE
as the sun is to shine; it being the most delightful and
natural employment of the Soul of Man: without
which you are dark and miserable. Consider therefore
the extent of Love, its vigour and excellency. For certainly he that delights not in Love makes vain the universe, and is of necessity to himself the greatest burden.
The whole world ministers to you as the theatre of
your Love. It sustains you and all objects that you may
continue to love them. Without which it were better
for you to have no being.

That violence wherewith
sometimes a man doteth upon one creature is but a
little spark of that love, even towards all, which lurketh
in his nature. We are made to love, both to satisfy the
necessity of our active nature, and to answer the beauties in every creature. By Love our Souls are married
and solder'd to [those of] the creatures: and it is our
Duty like God to be united to them all. We must love
them infinitely, but in God, and for God; and God in
them: namely all his excellencies manifested in them.
When we dote upon the perfections and beauties of
some one creature, we do not love that too much, but

[3]

other things too little. Never was anything in this world loved too much, but many things have been loved in a false way: and all in too short a measure.

2

A̲LL THEIR LIFE WAS SPENT
not in lawes, statutes or rules, but according to their
own free will and pleasure. They rose out of their beds
when they thought good: they did eat, drink, labour,
sleep, when they had a minde to it, and were disposed
for it. None did awake them, none did offer to constrain them to eat, drink, nor to do any other thing;
for so had Gargantua established it. In all their rule,
and strictest tie of their order, there was but this one
clause to be observed,

DO WHAT THOU WILT.

Because men that are free, well-borne, well-bred, and
conversant in honest companies, have naturally an
instinct and spurre (which is called honour) that
prompteth them unto vertuous actions, and withdraws
them from vice. Those same men, when by base sub-
jection and constraint they are brought under and
kept down, turn aside from that noble disposition, by
which they formerly were inclined to vertue, to shake
off and break that bond of servitude, wherein they are
so tyrannously inslaved; for it is agreeable with the
nature of man to long after things forbidden, and to
desire what is denied us.

3

Though I speak with the tongues of men and of angels, and have not charitie, I am become as sounding brasse or a tinkling cymbal. And though I have the gift of prophesie, and understand all mysteries and all knowledge: and though I have all faith, so that I could remove mountaines, and have not charitie, I am nothing. And though I bestowe all my goods to feed the poore, and though I give my body to bee burned, and have not charitie, it profiteth me nothing. Charitie suffereth long, and is kinde: charitie envieth not: charitie vaunteth not itselfe, is not puffed up, doth not behave itselfe unseemly; seeketh not her owne, is not easily provoked, thinketh no evill; rejoyceth not in iniquitie, but rejoyceth in the truth: beareth all things, beleeveth all things, hopeth all things, endureth all things. Charitie never faileth: but whether there be prophesies *they* shall faile; whether there bee tongues, *they* shall cease; whether there bee knowledge, *it* shall vanish away. For we know in part, and we prophesy in part. But when that which is perfect is come, then that which is in part shall be done away. When I was a childe, I spake as a childe, I understood as a childe, I thought

[6]

as a childe: but when I became a man I put away child-
ish things. For now we see through a glasse, darkely:
but then face to face: now I know in part, but then
shall I know even as also I am knowen. And now abid-
eth faith, hope, charitie, these three: but the greatest
of these is charitie.

4

Aʟʟ ʙɪʙʟᴇs ᴏʀ sᴀᴄʀᴇᴅ codes have been the causes of the following Errors:

1. That Man has two real existing principles: Viz: a Body and a Soul.

2. That Energy, call'd Evil, is alone from the Body; and that Reason, call'd Good, is alone from the Soul.

3. That God will torment Man in Eternity for following his Energies.

But the following Contraries to these are True:

1. Man has no Body distinct from his Soul; for that call'd Body is a portion of Soul discern'd by the five Senses, the chief inlets of Soul in this age.

2. Energy is the only life, and is from the Body; and Reason is the Bound or outward circumference of Energy.

3. Energy is Eternal Delight.

[8]

5

Jesus saith:
 The key of knowledge ye
hid: ye yourselves entered not in, and to them that
would enter in ye opened not.
 Let him that seeketh cease
not till he find. When he finds he shall be astonished:
astonished he shall reach the kingdom: and having
reached the kingdom he shall rest.
 The kingdom of heaven is
within you: and whosoever knoweth himself shall find
it.
 Raise the stone and thou
shalt find me. Cleave the wood and I am there.

6

THEY THAT LOVE BEYOND
the world cannot be separated by it.

Death cannot kill what
never dies.

Nor can spirits ever be
divided, that love and live in the same principle; the
root and record of their friendship.

If absence be not death,
neither is theirs.

Death is but crossing the
world, as friends do the seas; they live in one another
still.

For they must needs be
present, that love and live in that which is omnipres-
ent.

In this divine glass they see
face to face; and their converse is free . . .

This is the comfort of
friends, that though they may be said to die, yet their
friendship and society are, in the best sense, ever present, because immortal.

7

THERE IS A SPIRIT, WHICH
I feel, that delights to do no Evil, nor to revenge any
Wrong, but delights to endure all things, in hope to
enjoy its own in the End: Its hope is to outlive all
Wrath and Contention, and to weary out all Exalta-
tion and Cruelty, or whatever is of a Nature contrary
to itself. It sees to the End of all Temptations: As it
bears no Evil in itself, so it conceives none in Thoughts
to any other: If it be betrayed it bears it; for its Ground
and Spring is the Mercies and Forgiveness of God. Its
Crown is Meekness, its Life is Everlasting Love un-
feigned. It takes its Kingdom with Intreaty and not
with Contention, and keeps it by lowliness of Mind.
In God alone it can rejoyce, though none else regard
it, or can own its Life. It's conceived in Sorrow, and
brought forth without any to pity it; nor doth it mur-
mur at Grief and Oppression. I found it alone, being
forsaken; I have Fellowship therein with them who
lived in Dens and desolate places in the Earth, who
through Death obtained this Resurrection and Eternal
Holy Life.

8

THE ANCIENT POETS ANI-
mated all sensible objects with Gods or Geniuses,
calling them by the names and adorning them with the
properties of woods, rivers, mountains, lakes, cities,
nations, and whatever their enlarged and numerous
senses could perceive.

And particularly they stud-
ied the genius of each city and country, placing it
under its mental deity;

Till a system was formed,
which some took advantage of, and enslaved the vulgar
by attempting to realize or abstract the mental deities
from their objects: thus began Priesthood;

Choosing forms of worship
from poetic tales.

And at length they pro-
nounc'd that the Gods had ordered such things.

Thus men forgot that all
deities reside in the human breast.

9

B ELOVED, LET US LOVE ONE
another: for love is of God.

He that loveth not knoweth
not God; for God is love.

God is love; and he that
dwelleth in love dwelleth in God, and God in him.

Perfect love casteth out
fear.

10

A FLOWER HAS OPENED IN MY HEART . . .
What flower is this, what flower of spring,
What simple, secret thing?
It is the peace that shines apart,
The peace of daybreak skies that bring
Clear song and wild swift wing.

Heart's miracle of inward light,
What powers unknown have sown your seed
And your perfection freed? . . .
O flower within me wondrous white,
I know you only as my need
And my unsealèd sight.

11

THE WORLD IS BEST EN-
joyed and most immediately while we converse bless-
edly and wisely with men. I am sure it were desirable
that they could give and receive infinite treasures: and
perhaps they can. For whomsoever I love as myself, to
him I give myself, and all my happiness, which I think
is infinite: and I receive him and all his happiness. Yes,
in him I receive God, for God delighteth me for being
his blessedness: so that a man obligeth me infinitely
that maketh himself happy; and by making himself
happy, giveth me himself and all his happiness.

12

THE KINDLY MARITORNES loved greatly, in her own way, and should be pardoned for her affairs with carriers since she indulged them out of pure softness of heart. You may well believe that the bountiful Asturian wench sought rather to give than receive pleasure; if she yielded her person, it was, as happens to not a few Maritornes, in order not to see men fret and suffer. She wished to purify the carriers of the base desires that soiled their minds, and to leave them clean for their work. 'She plumed herself greatly on being a lady', says Cervantes, and in that quality she had arranged to visit the carrier 'and meet his wishes unreservedly', not satisfy hers. And for this simple selflessness, as free from taint of vice as from namby-pamby innocence, the Asturian girl has been immortalized. She lived beyond both innocence and the mischief caused by its loss.

13

To SEE A WORLD IN A GRAIN OF SAND
And a Heaven in a Wild Flower,
Hold Infinity in the palm of your hand,
And Eternity in an hour.

A Robin Redbreast in a Cage
Puts all Heaven in a Rage.

Each outcry of the hunted Hare
A fibre from the Brain does tear.

The Catterpillar on the Leaf
Repeats to thee thy Mother's grief.

Joy and Woe are woven fine,
A clothing for the Soul divine.

The Soldier, arm'd with Sword and Gun,
Palsied strikes the Summer's Sun.

If the Sun and Moon should doubt,
They'd immediately go out.

14

CHRISTIAN CHARITY IS
Friendship to all the world; and when friendships
were the noblest things in the world, Charity was little, like the Sunne drawn in at a chinke, or his beames
drawn into the Centre of a Burning-glasse; but *Christian* charity is friendship expanded like the face of the
sunne when it mounts above the eastern hills: and I
was strangely pleas'd when I saw something of this in
Cicero . . . Nature hath made friendships and socie-
ties, relations and endearments; and by something or
other we relate to all the world; there is enough in
every man that is willing to make him become our
friend; but when men *contract* friendships they enclose the Commons; and what Nature intended should
be every man's, we make proper to two or three.
Friendship is, like rivers and the strand of seas, and the
ayre, common to all the world; but Tyrants, and evil
customes, warrs, and want of love, have made them
proper and peculiar.

15

I ASK MYSELF SOMETIMES,
is not morality a worse enemy of spirit than immoral-
ity? Is it not more hopelessly deceptive and entangling?
Those romantic poets, for instance, whose lives were
often so irregular—were they not evidently far more
spiritual than the good people whom they shocked?
Shelley, Leopardi, Alfred de Musset were essentially
children of the spirit; they were condemned to flutter
on broken wings only for lack of measure and discipline; they were spiritual waifs, untaught to see the
relativity and absurdity of their proud passions. The
perfect spirit must be a patient hearer, a sober pupil,
not an occasional automatic skylark. Yet when spiritu-
ality, as in Wordsworth, has to struggle instead against
a black coat and a white choker, it seems to be more
sadly and decisively stifled, buried alive under a mountain of human alarms and a heavy tombstone of sancti-
mony. The world, he sighed, is too much with us; but
the hills and even the mock Tritons blowing their
wreathed horns were not able to banish the world from
his conscientious concern. Nothing is able to banish
the world except contempt for the world, and this was
not in him. It would even have been contrary to his

Protestant religion—that so unspiritual determination to wash the world white and clean, adopt it, and set it up for a respectable person. The world is not respectable; it is mortal, tormented, confused, deluded for ever; but it is shot through with beauty, with love, with glints of courage and laughter; and in these the spirit blooms timidly, and struggles to the light among the thorns.

16

IN ONE SOUL WE MAY BE entertained and taken up with innumerable beauties. But in the Soul of Man there are innumerable infinities. One soul in the immensity of its intelligence is greater and more excellent than the whole world. The Ocean is but the drop of a bucket to it, the Heavens but a centre, the Sun obscurity, and all Ages but as one day; it being by its understanding a Temple of Eternity, and God's omnipresence, between which and the whole world there is no proportion. Its Love is a dominion greater than that which Adam had in Paradise: and yet the fruition of it is but solitary. We need spectators, and other diversities of friends and lovers, in whose souls we might likewise dwell, and with whose beauties we might be crowned, and entertained: in all whom we can dwell exactly, and be present with them fully. Lest therefore the other depths and faculties of our souls should be desolate and idle, they also are created to entertain us. And as in many mirrors we are so many other selves, so are we spiritually multiplied when we meet ourselves more sweetly, and live again, in other persons.

17

Ah sunflower, weary of time,
Who countest the steps of the Sun,
Seeking after that sweet golden clime
Where the traveller's journey is done:

Where the Youth, pined away with desire,
And the pale Virgin, shrouded in snow,
Arise from their graves and aspire
Where my Sunflower wishes to go.

18

OF THE 'REAL' UNIVERSE we know nothing, except that there exist as many versions of it as there are perceptive minds. Each man lives alone in his private universe, a system closed and confined within the ever-widening circle of his consciousness: 'we live, as we dream, apart'. Yet it is easy to make too much of this purely logical impediment to the marriage of true minds; for that they desire each other at all suggests an already existing community between them. Like calls to like; the vibration of identity subdues the logic of difference; and it may be that the spirit's isolation in the ego is no more than the last illusion that shall be conquered. Love between human beings springs from a desire to be made free of another world than one's own; every true communion of lovers is a mutual discovery and recognition: every passion is a passion for release, for that loss of one's self by which alone one gains life.

19

Be not disheartened by the misdoing of men. Love a man even in his misdoing, for such love is a likeness of the divine, and the highest we can know on earth. Love all God's creation, both the whole and every grain of sand. Love every leaf, every ray of light. Love the animals, love the plants, love every several thing. By love you shall discern God's mystery quickening all things, and so, day by day, be drawn into a fuller understanding of it: till at last you will come to love the whole world with an all-embracing love.

Sometimes, at the sight of men's misdoing, one stands perplexed, wondering how to correct it, whether by coercion or by love. Let all things be done in love and humility. If to that resolve we hold fast, we shall win all the world to our heart's persuasion.

20

THE WHOLE WORLD BE-
fore thee is as a little graine of the ballance: yea, as a
drop of the morning dew that falleth down upon the
earth. But thou hast mercy upon all; for thou canst
doe all things, and winkest at the sinnes of men, because they should amend. For thou lovest all the things
that are, and abhorrest nothing which thou hast made:
for never wouldst thou have made anything if thou
hadst hated it. And how could anything have endured
if it had not been thy will? or been preserved, if not
called by thee? But thou sparest all: for they are thine
—O Lord thou lover of souls. For thine incorruptible
Spirit is in all things.

21

Iᴛ ᴡᴇʀᴇ ʙᴇᴛᴛᴇʀ ᴛᴏ ʜᴀᴠᴇ
no opinion of God at all, than such an opinion as is
unworthy of him: for the one is unbelief, the other is
contumely: and certainly superstition is the reproach
of the Deity. Plutarch saith well to that purpose:
'Surely', saith he, 'I had rather a great deal men should
say, that there was no such man at all as Plutarch, than
that they should say, that there was one Plutarch, that
would eat his children as soon as they were born; as
the poets speak of Saturn'. And as the contumely is
greater towards God, so the danger is greater towards
men. Atheism leaves a man to sense, to philosophy, to
natural piety, to laws, to reputation; all which may be
guides to an outward moral virtue, though religion
were not: but superstition dismounts all these, and
erecteth an absolute monarchy in the minds of men.
Therefore atheism did never perturb states; for it
makes men wary of themselves, as looking no further:
and we see the times inclined to atheism, as the time
of Augustus Caesar, were civil times. But superstition
hath been the confusion of many states; and bringeth
in a new primum mobile, that ravisheth all the spheres
of government.

22

THE THOUGHT OF OUR PAST YEARS IN ME DOTH BREED
Perpetual benediction: not indeed
For that which is most worthy to be blest—
Delight and liberty, the simple creed
Of childhood, whether busy or at rest,
With new-fledged hope still fluttering in his breast—
　　　Not for these I raise
　　　The song of thanks and praise;
　　But for those obstinate questionings
　　Of sense and outward things;
　　Fallings from us, vanishings;
　　Blank misgivings of a Creature
Moving about in worlds not realized;
High instincts before which our mortal Nature
Did tremble like a guilty thing surprised:
　　　But for those first affections,
　　　Those shadowy recollections,
　　Which, be they what they may,
Are yet the fountain light of all our day,
Are yet a master light of all our seeing;
　　Uphold us, cherish, and have power to make
Our noisy years seem moments in the being
Of the eternal Silence.

[27]

23

THERE IS A CERTAIN WIS-
dom of humanity which is common to the greatest men
with the lowest, and which our ordinary education
often labours to silence and obstruct. The mind is one;
and the best minds who love truth for its own sake,
think much less of property in truth. Thankfully they
accept it everywhere, and do not label or stamp it with
any man's name, for it is theirs long beforehand. It is
theirs from eternity. The learned and the studious of
thought have no monopoly of wisdom. Their violence
of direction in some degree disqualifies them to think
truly. We owe many valuable observations to people
who are not very acute or profound, and who say the
thing without effort, which we want and have long
been hunting in vain. The action of the soul is oftener
in that which is felt and left unsaid, than in that which
is said in any conversation. It broods over every society,
and they unconsciously seek for it in each other. We
know better than we do. We do not yet possess ourselves, and we know at the same time that we are much
more. I feel the same truth how often in my trivial
conversation with my neighbours, that somewhat
higher in each of us overlooks this by-play, and Jove
nods to Jove from behind each of us.

24

Do I COUNSEL YOU TO SLAY your instincts? I counsel you to innocence of the instincts.

Do I counsel you to chastity? Chastity is a virtue in some, but in many almost a vice.

These, it is true, are abstinent; but from all that they do the she-dog of sensuality looks out with envious eyes.

To the very heights of their virtue, and to the depths of their cold spirit, this monster pads after them, bringing disquiet.

And how cunningly this she-dog can beg for a piece of spirit if a piece of flesh is denied to it.

Do you love tragic events and all things that break the heart? I mistrust your she-dog.

Your eyes are too cruel for me, and you look about you with lusting glances, seeking those who shall suffer. Is not your sensuality borrowing for itself the guise and name of compassion?

He to whom chastity is difficult should be dissuaded from it: lest it become for him the way to hell—mire and lust in the soul.

25

My wits are not enough
To take this evening flame
And forge in it the stuff
Of song without a name,
An April lyric clean
As the orchard grass is green,
Shining as the bright
April evening light.
I have not yet lived long
Enough to be so young
As the old innocence
Of the eternal Spring.

26

LOOK THOU WITHIN: WITH-
in thee is the fountain of all good, whose waters shall
never cease to spring, so thou dig deep enough. No
soul is willingly bereaved of Truth, nor of those natural inclinations to justice and equanimity and kindness that are the fruit of her knowledge. It is most
needful that thou remember this always: so shalt thou
be far more gentle both in thy disposition towards men
and in thy commerce with them. The true joy of man
is in doing that which is most proper to his nature; and
the first property of man is to be kindly affected towards them that are of one kind with himself. Let this,
therefore, be thy sole care and desire: so always and in
all things to conduct thyself, whether doing or for-
bearing, as the law of charity and kind doth require.

27

THE BODY IS THE TEMPLE of the Holy Spirit, and is the means whereby alone the soul can establish relation with the universe which constitutes man's earthly environment. To regard the body, or any part of it, or any of its natural function-ings, as indecent or vile is therefore to fall into the sin of impiety. Men and women are furnished with many mysterious faculties which we must assume are pur-posive—intended for use. We are guided as to their right exercise by what the psychologists call emotional reactions. These reactions, however, often clash, and so we are further equipped with a balancing faculty called reason or intellect. No emotion is more potent or more 'ennobling' (as measured by our religious ideals) than that which marks love between man and woman. The valuable essence of love is non-material, but, in fulfillment of the divine purpose, this is often interfused with an impulse towards a physical expres-sion in itself natural and spiritually illuminating. The beauty of love, however, vanishes if its mere physical expression be consciously sought as a means of sensual gratification, without the spiritual and aesthetic ac-companiments that alone give it human value. This is as true within as without marriage . . . Purity in sex relations is a matter of conscience and good taste— spiritual and aesthetic; not of law-courts or of ethical dogmas laid down by regenerate monks or ecclesiastic pundits.

28

AND ERLY IN THE MORN-
ing came Jesus agayne into the temple; and all the
people came unto him; and he sate doune and taught
them. And the scribes and the Pharisees brought unto
him a woman taken in adultery, and sett her in the
middes, and sayde unto him: Master, this woman was
taken in adultery, even as the dede was a-doing. Now
Moses in the lawe commanded us that such shoulde
be stoned: what then sayest thou of her? This they
sayde tempting him, that they might have whereof to
accuse him. And Jesus stouped doune, and with his
finger wrote on the grounde. But when they continued
axing him, he lifted himself up and sayde unto them:
Lett him that is without sin among you cast the first
stone. And agayne he stouped doune and wrote on the
grounde. And they, when they herde that, went out
won by won, the eldest first.

29

THERE IS NOT ONE MORAL
Virtue that Jesus inculcated but Plato and Cicero did
inculcate before him. What then did Christ inculcate?
Forgiveness of Sins. This alone is the Gospel, and this
is the Life and Immortality brought to light by Jesus,
even the Covenant of Jehovah, which is this: If you
forgive one another your Trespasses, so shall Jehovah
forgive you, that he himself may dwell among you; but
if you avenge, you murder the Divine Image, and he
cannot dwell among you; because you murder him he
arises again, and you deny that he is arisen, and are
blind to Spirit.

30

A̲LL THIS HEMISPHERE OF
the world [said Gargantua to his vanquished enemies]
was filled with the praises and congratulations which
your selves and your fathers made, when Alpharbal
King of Canarre, not satisfied with his own fortunes,
did most furiously invade the land of Onyx, and with
cruel Piracies molest all the Armorick islands, and
confine regions of Britanie; yet was he in a set naval
fight justly taken and vanquished by my father, whom
God preserve and protect. But what? whereas other
Kings and Emperours, yea those who entitle themselves Catholiques, would have dealt roughly with
him, kept him a close prisoner, and put him to an ex-
tream high ransom: he [my father] intreated him very
courteously, lodged him kindly with himself in his
own Palace, and out of his incredible mildnesse and
gentle disposition sent him back with a safe conduct,
loaden with gifts, loaden with favours, loaden with all
offices of friendship. What fell out upon it? Being returned into his countrey, he [Alpharbal] called a
Parliament, where all the Princes and States of his
Kingdom being assembled, he shewed them the humanity which he had found in us, and therefore wished

them to take such course by way of compensation therein, as that the whole world might be edified by the example, as well of their honest graciousnesse to us, as of our gracious honesty towards them. The result hereof was, that it was voted and decreed by a unanimous consent, that they should offer up entirely their Lands, Dominions and Kingdomes, to be disposed of by us according to our pleasure.

Alpharbal in his own person, presently returned. . . . Being safely arrived, he came to my said father, and would have kist his feet: that action was found too submissively low, and therefore was not permitted, but in exchange he was most cordially embraced: he offered his presents, they were not received, because they were too excessive: he yielded himself voluntarily a servant and vassal, and was content his whole posterity should be liable to the same bondage; and this was not accepted of, because it seemed not equitable: he surrendered by vertue of the decree of his great Parliamentarie councel, his whole Countreys and Kingdomes to him, offering the Deed and Conveyance, signed, sealed and ratified by all those that were concerned in it; this was altogether refused, and the parchments cast into the fire. In end, this free good will and simple meaning of the Canarriens wrought such tendernesse in my father's heart, that he could not abstain from shedding teares, and wept most profusely: then, by choice words very congruously adapted, strove in what he could to diminish the estimation of the good offices which he had done them, saying, that any courtesie he had conferred upon them was not worth a rush, and what favour so ever he had shewed them, he was bound to do it. . . . This is the nature of gratitude and true thankfulnesse. For time, which gnawes and diminisheth all things else, augments and increaseth benefits; because a noble action of liberality, done to a man of reason, doth grow continually, by his generous thinking of it and remembering it.

Being unwilling therefore any way to degenerate from the hereditary mildnesse and clemencie of my Parents, I do now forgive you, deliver you from all fines and imprisonments, fully release you, set you at liberty, and every way make you as frank and free as ever you were before. . . .

31

IN THE BEGINNING WAS IMAGINATION:
   in the beginning was the Seed.
      And the Seed was in God:
      and the Seed is God.
   All things are the flowering of That.

In the Seed was that Light
   which lighteth every man
that cometh into the world.
The Light shineth in darkness,
   and the darkness overpowers it not.

32

―――――――――――――――――――――――

THE FIRST THING THAT hinders the prayer of a good man from obtaining its effect is a violent anger, a violent storm in the spirit of him that prayes. For anger sets the house on fire, and all the spirits are busie upon trouble, and intend propulsion, defence, displeasure or revenge; it is a short madness, and an eternal enemy to discourse and sober counsels and fair conversation; it intends its own object with all the earnestness of perception or activity of design, and a quicker motion of a too warm and distempered bloud; it is a fever in the heart, and a calenture in the head, and a fire in the face, and a sword in the hand, and a fury all over; and therefore can never suffer a man to be in a disposition to pray. For prayer is an action and a state of entercourse and desire, exactly contrary to the character of anger. Prayer is an action of likeness to the holy Ghost, the Spirit of gentleness and dove-like simplicity . . . the peace of our spirit and the stilness of our thoughts, the evenness of recollection, the seat of meditation, the rest of our cares and the calme of our tempest: prayer is the issue of a quiet minde, of untroubled thoughts; it is the daughter of charity and the sister of meekness; and he that prayes to God with an angry, that is, with a troubled and discomposed spirit, is like him that retires into a battle to meditate, and sets up his closet in the out quarters of an army, and chuses a frontier garrison to be wise in. Anger is a perfect alienation of the minde from prayer.

33

By the word soul, or psyche, I mean that inner consciousness which aspires. By prayer I do not mean a request preferred to a deity; I mean . . . intense aspiration.

34

SPIRIT IS AWARENESS, IN-
telligence, recollection. It requires no dogmas, as does
animal faith or the art of living. Human morality, for
the spirit, is but the inevitable and hygienic bias of one
race of animals. Spirit itself is not human; it may
spring up in any life; it may detach itself from any
provincialism; as it exists in all nations and religions,
so it may exist in all animals, and who knows in how
many undreamt-of beings, and in the midst of what
worlds? It might flourish, as the Stoics felt, even in the
face of chaos, except that chaos could not sustain the
animal life, the psyche, which spirit requires for its
organ. From the existence of spirit a psychologist may
therefore argue back to the existence—at least local
and temporary—of some cosmos of organized matter:
but this dependence of mind on body is a lesson taught
by natural philosophy, when natural philosophy is
sound; it is not a free or evident requirement of spirit
in its first deliverance. On the contrary, the body which
is the matrix and cradle of spirit in time, seems a
stumbling-block to it in its spontaneous career; and
a rather long discipline and much chastening hardly
persuade this supernatural nursling that it is really so

domestic, and that it borrows its existence from a poor, busy, precarious animal life; or that the natural rhythms, pauses, and synthetic reactions of that life are the ground of its native affinity with the eternal.

35

W<small>E ARE APT TO LOVE</small> praise, but not to deserve it. But if we would deserve it, we must love virtue more than that.

Be not fond, therefore, of praise; but seek virtue that leads to it.

And yet no more lessen or dissemble thy merit, than overrate it; for though humility be a virtue, an affected one is none.

36

ALL'S IN THIS FLOWER . . .
Times, seasons, losses, all the fruits of woe,
Beauty's fragility, and death's bare gain,
Pluck'd in passing by, five minutes ago.

All's in this flower, the war of life and death,
God's character and purpose written down,
The force of love, the proof and power of faith—
All's here, and all unknown.

37

I DO NOT SEE HOW A MAN without sincerity can be good for anything. How can a cart or carriage be made to go without yoke or cross-bar?

When you see a good man, think of emulating him; when you see a bad man, examine your own heart.

Without due self-restraint, courtesy becomes oppressive, prudence degenerates into timidity, valour into violence, and candour into rudeness.

Men's natures are alike; it is their habits that carry them far apart.

Your goody-goody people are the thieves of virtue.

That virtue is perfect which adheres to a constant mean. It has long been rare amongst men.

True goodness springs from a man's own heart. All men are born good.

38

W HAT *is* SINCERITY? IT IS
something more than a refraining from lies and dis-
simulation: something that can only be achieved by
a drastic purging of oneself. We are too ready to pan-
der, even in the quiet of our private mind, to our
moral vanities and false shames, persuading ourselves
that we think and feel and desire as—in deference to
some accepted opinion or moral ideal—we fancy we
ought to think and feel and desire. To be rid of this
'ought', to accept ourselves with candour, is the first
condition of sane and honest living. Sincerity begins
at home, in one's own heart. Without self-knowledge
it cannot exist, and self-knowledge is not easily won
by minds in which a diseased notion of what constitutes
'sin' has found a breeding-place. Modern psychology,
though it is the source of some new confusions as well
as of much enlightenment, has at least left us with no
excuse for supposing our ostensible motives and our
real motives to be always identical. Self-deception, the
first and last enemy of the good (which is the reasonable) life, has always been the favourite resort of the
maladjusted psyche. 'Your only true virtue', says
Nietzsche, 'is your dearest self'. There is a positive

[49]

danger, as well as falsehood, in attempting to conform to an ideal of virtue that is alien to the deepest impulses of one's own spirit. Given intelligence and spiritual tact, all that is done is well done.

39

THE PRIMARY AND SOLE
foundation of virtue or of the proper conduct of life
is to seek our own profit.

Blessedness is not the reward of virtue, but is virtue itself.

40

THE WHOLE OUTWARD VIS-
ible world with all its being is a signature or figure
of the inward spiritual world; whatever is internally,
and however its operation is, so likewise it has its character externally; like as the spirit of each creature sets
forth and manifests the internal form of its birth by its
body, so does the Eternal Being also.

The Being of all beings is a
wrestling power.

The spirit is signed in the
body: whatever the spirit is in itself in an incompre-
hensible operation, the same is the body in the com-
prehensible and visible working.

There is not anything but
it has its soul in it according to its property, and the
soul is a kernel to another body. Whatever lives and
grows has its seed in it; God has comprehended all
things in his word, and spoken them forth into a form.
The speaking works in itself, viz. in the eternity, and
the spoken also in itself, viz. in the time; the speaking
is the master, and the spoken is the instrument; the
speaking makes the nature of eternity, and the spoken
makes the nature of time.

41

To LIVE HAPPILY IS AN IN-
ward power of the soul when she is affected with
indifferency towards those things that are by their
nature indifferent. To be thus affected she must consider all worldly objects both divided and whole:
remembering withal that no object can of itself beget
any opinion in us, neither can come to us, but stands
without, still and quiet; but that we ourselves beget,
and as it were print in ourselves, opinions concerning
them. Now it is in our power not to print them; and,
if they creep in and lurk in some corner, it is in our
power to wipe them off. Remember, moreover, that
this care and circumspection of thine is to continue
but for a while, and then thy life will be at an end.
And what should hinder but that thou mayest do well
with all these things? For if they be according to
nature, rejoice in them, and let them be pleasing and
acceptable unto thee. But if they be against nature,
seek thou that which is according to thine own nature,
and, whether it be for thy credit or no, use all possible
speed for the attainment of it: for no man ought to be
blamed for seeking his own good and happiness.

42

From the same source as gentleness comes that spirit by whose virtue a man will oppose a loving countenance and friendly speech, and all the effects of understanding, to those who cherish anger against him. It is by the operation of kindness that charity herself lives and bears fruit in a man; for the heart plenished with kindness is like a lamp filled with precious oil. By its fair example, kindness enlightens the misdoer, and by its good offices it brings healing to those hearts that are hurt, grieved, or vext. Them that have charity it maketh to burn and shine, and in its flame neither jealousy nor envy may endure.

43

SING BRAVELY IN MY HEART, YOU PATIENT BIRDS
Who all this weary winter wait for spring;
Sing, till such wonder wakens in my words
As I have known long since, beyond all voicing,—
Strong with the beat of blood, wild on the wing,
Rebellious and rejoicing.

Watch with me, inward solemn influence,
Invisible, intangible, unkenned;
Wind of the darkness that shall bear me hence;
O life within my life, flame within flame,
Who mak'st me one with song that has no end,
And with that stillness whence my spirit came.

44

TRUE RELIGION DOTH CLEAR the mind from all impotent and unsatiable desires, which do abuse and toss a man's soul, and make it restless and unquiet. It sets a man free from eager and impetuous loves, and by these men are torn in pieces; from vain and disappointing hopes, which sink men into melancholy; from lawless and exorbitant appetites; from frothy and empty joys; from dismal, presaging fears, and anxious, self-devouring cares; from inward heartburnings; from self-eating envy; from swelling pride and ambition; from dull and black melancholy; from boiling anger and raging fury; from a gnawing, aching conscience; from an arbitrary presumption; from rigid sourness and severity of spirit;— for these make the man that is not biased and principled with religion to seethe like a pot, inwardly to boil with the fire and pitchy fumes of hell, and as outrageous as when the great leviathan doth cause the waves of the sea to cast out mire and dirt.

45

P RAY, WHAT IS THE VIRTUE,
the power, the height and the greatness of love?

The virtue of love is NOTH-
ING and ALL, or that nothing visible out of which all
things proceed; its power is through all things; its
height is as high as God; its greatness is as great as God.
Its virtue is the principle of all principles; its power
supports the heavens and upholds the earth; its height
is higher than the highest heavens; and its greatness is
even greater than the very manifestation of the God-
head in the glorious light of the divine essence, as being
infinitely capable of greater and greater manifestations
in all eternity. Love, being the highest principle, is the
virtue of all virtues; from whence they flow forth. Love,
being the greatest majesty, is the power of all powers,
from whence they severally operate: And it is the holy
magical root, or ghostly power, from whence all the
wonders of God have been wrought by the hands of
his elect servants, in all their generations successively.
Whosoever finds it, finds nothing and all things.

Dear master, pray tell me
but how I may understand this.

First, then, in that I said,

'Its virtue is nothing', or that nothing which is the beginning of all things, thou must understand it thus: When thou art gone forth wholly from the creature, and from that which is visible, and art become nothing to all that is nature and creature, then thou art in that Eternal One which is God himself: And then thou shalt perceive and feel in thy interior the highest virtue of love. But in that I said 'Its power is through all things', this is that which thou perceivest and findest in thy own soul and body experimentally, whenever this great love is enkindled within thee. Thou shalt then see how love hath poured forth itself into all things, and penetrateth all things, and is the most inward and most outward ground in all things: Inwardly in the virtue and power of everything, and outwardly in the figure and form thereof. And in that I also said, 'Its greatness is as great as God', thou art hereby to understand that there is a certain greatness and lattitude of heart in love, which is inexpressible; for it enlarges the soul as wide as the whole creation of God. And this shall be truly experienced by thee, beyond all words, when the throne of love shall be set up in thy heart. And in that I lastly said, 'Whosoever finds it, finds all things', there is nothing can be more true than this assertion. It hath been the beginning of all things; and it ruleth all things. It is also the end of all things; and will thence comprehend all things within its circle. All things are from it, and in it, and by it. If thou findest it, thou comest into that ground whence all things are proceeded, and wherein they subsist; and thou art in it a King over all the works of God.

46

FOR LOVE DOTH USE US FOR A SOUND OF SONG,
And Love's meaning our life wields,
Making our souls like syllables to throng
His tunes of exultation.

Down the blind speed of a fatal world we fly,
As rain blown along earth's fields;
Yet are we god-desiring liturgy,
Sung songs of adoration;

Yea, made of chance and all a labouring strife,
We go charged with a strong flame;
For as a language Love hath seized on life
His burning heart to story.

Yea, Love, we are thine, the liturgy of thee,
Thy thought's golden and glad name,
The mortal conscience of immortal glee,
Love's zeal in Love's own glory.

47

T RUE KNOWLEDGE IS MOD-
est and wary; tis ignorance that is bold and presuming.
They that never peeped beyond the common belief in
which their easie understandings were first indoctri-
nated, are strongly assured of the truth and compara-
tive excellency of their receptions; while the larger
souls that have travelled the divers climates of opinions
are more cautious in their resolves, and more sparing
to determine.

48

HE THAT HAS GROWN TO WISDOM HURRIES NOT,
  But thinks and weighs what Reason bids him do;
And after thinking he retains his thought
  Until as he conceived the fact ensue.
Let no man to o'erweening pride be wrought,
  But count his state as fortune's gift and due.
He is a fool who deems that none has sought
  The truth, save he alone, or knows it true.
Many strange birds are on the air abroad,
  Nor are all of one flight or of one force,
    But each after his kind dissimilar:
To each was portion'd of the breath of God,
  Who gave them divers instincts from one source.
    Then judge not thou thy fellows what they are.

49

LOVE BE IN MY HEAD, AND in my understanding. Love be in mine eyes and in my looking. Love be in my mouth and in my speaking. Love be in my heart and in my thinking. Love be at mine end, and at my departing.

50

ALL OUR TROUBLE IS from within us; and if a dish of lettice and a clear fountain can cool all my heats, so that I shall have neither thirst nor pride, lust nor revenge, envie nor ambition, I am lodg'd in the bosome of felicity; and indeed no men sleep so soundly as they that lay their head upon Natures lap. For a single dish and a clean chalice lifted from the springs can cure my hunger and thirst: but the meat of Ahasuerus feast cannot satisfie my ambition and my pride. He therefore that hath the fewest desires and the most quiet passions, whose wants are soon provided for and whose possessions cannot be disturbed with violent fears, he that dwels next door to satisfaction and can carry his needs and lay them down where hee please, this man is the happy man, and this is not to be done in great designes and swelling fortunes.

51

Thou, whose exterior semblance doth belie
     Thy Soul's immensity;
Thou best Philosopher, who yet dost keep
Thy heritage, thou Eye among the blind,
That deaf and silent, read'st the eternal deep,
Haunted for ever by the eternal mind—
     Mighty Prophet! Seer blest!
     On whom those truths do rest
Which we are toiling all our lives to find,
In darkness lost, the darkness of the grave;
Thou, over whom thy Immortality
Broods like the Day, a Master o'er a slave,
A Presence which is not to be put by—
Thou little Child, yet glorious in the might
Of heaven-born freedom . . .

52

FERVENT BELIEVERS LOOK for some system of philosophy or religion that shall be *literally* true and worthy of superseding the current assumptions of daily life. I look for no such thing. Never for a moment can I bring myself to regard a human system—a piece of mental discourse—as more than a system of notation, sometimes picturesque, sometimes abstract and mathematical. Scientific symbols, terms in which calculation is possible, may replace poetic symbols, which merely catch echoes of the senses or make up dramatic units out of appearances in the gross. But the most accurate scientific system would still be only a method of description, and the actual facts would continue to rejoice in their own ways of being. The relevance and truth of science, like the relevance and truth of sense, are pragmatic, in that they mark the actual relations, march, and distribution of events, in the terms in which they enter our experience.

53

O GOD, WHO ART THE
author of peace and lover of concord, in knowledge of
whom standeth our eternal life, whose service is perfect freedom: defend us thy humble servants in all
assaults of our enemies; that we, surely trusting in thy
defence, may not fear the power of any adversaries.

O God, from whom all holy
desires, all good counsels, and all just works do proceed: Give unto thy servants that peace which the
world cannot give; that both our hearts may be set to
obey thy commandments, and also that by thee we
being defended from the fear of our enemies may pass
our time in rest and quietness.

54

THE RACE FLOWS THROUGH us, the race is the drama and we the incidents. This is not any sort of poetical statement; it is a statement of fact. In so far as we are individuals, in so far as we seek to follow merely individual ends, we are accidental, disconnected, without significance, the sport of chance. In so far as we realize ourselves as experiments of the species for the species, just in so far do we escape from the accidental and the chaotic. We are episodes in an experience greater than ourselves.

Now none of this, if you read me aright, makes for the suppression of one's individual difference, but it does make for its correlation. We have to get everything we can out of ourselves for this very reason that we do not stand alone; we signify as parts of a universal and immortal development. Our separate selves are our charges, the talents of which much has to be made. It is because we are episodical in the great synthesis of life that we have to make the utmost of our individual lives and traits and possibilities.

55

Is it the act of a just
man, I asked, to hurt anybody?

Certainly it is, he replied;
that is to say, it is his duty to hurt those who are both
wicked, and enemies of his.

Are horses made better, or
worse, by being hurt?

Worse.

Worse with reference to the
excellence of dogs, or that of horses?

That of horses.

Are dogs in the same way
made worse by being hurt, with reference to the excellence of dogs, and not of horses?

Unquestionably they are.

And must we not, on the
same principle, assert, my friend, that men, by being
hurt, are lowered in the scale of human excellence?

Indeed we must.

But is not justice a human
excellence?

Undoubtedly it is.

And therefore, my friend,

those men who are hurt must needs be rendered less just.

So it would seem.

Can musicians, by the art of music, make men unmusical?

They cannot.

Can riding-masters, by the art of riding, make men bad riders?

No.

But if so, can the just by justice make men unjust? In short, can the good by goodness make men bad?

No, it is impossible.

True; for, if I am not mistaken, it is the property, not of warmth, but of its opposite, to make things cold.

Yes.

And it is the property not of drought, but of its opposite, to make things wet.

Certainly.

Then it is the property not of good, but of its opposite, to hurt.

Apparently it is.

Well, is the just man good?

Certainly he is.

Then, Polemarchus, it is the property, not of the just man, but of his opposite, the unjust man, to hurt either friend or any other creature.

You seem to me to be perfectly right, Socrates.

Hence if anyone asserts that it is just to render to every man his due, and if he understands by this, that what is due on the part of the just man is injury to his enemies, and assistance to his friends, the assertion is that of an unwise man. For the doctrine is untrue; because we have discovered that in no instance is it just to injure anybody.

56

ABSTINENCE SOWS SAND ALL OVER
The ruddy limbs and flaming hair:
But Desire Gratified
Plants fruits of life and beauty there.

57

T HEY THAT SHALL OPPOSE
thee in thy right courses, as it is not in their power to
divert thee from thy good action, so neither let it be to
divert thee from thy good affection towards them. But
be it thy care to keep thyself constant in both; both in
a right judgment and action, and in true meekness
towards them that either shall do their endeavour to
hinder thee, or at least will be displeased with thee for
what thou hast done. For to fail in either (either in the
one to give over for fear, or in the other to forsake thy
natural affection towards him who by nature is both
thy friend and thy kinsman) is equally base, and much
savouring of the disposition of a cowardly fugitive
soldier.

58

A THING OF BEAUTY IS A JOY FOR EVER:
Its loveliness increases; it will never
Pass into nothingness; but still will keep
A bower quiet for us, and a sleep
Full of sweet dreams, and health, and quiet breathing.
Therefore on every morrow are we wreathing
A flowery band to bind us to the earth,
Spite of despondence, of the inhuman dearth
Of noble natures, of the gloomy days,
Of all the unhealthy and o'erdarkened ways
Made for our searching: yes, in spite of all,
Some shape of beauty moves away the pall
From our dark spirits.

59

FRIENDSHIP IS A UNION OF spirits, a marriage of hearts, and the bond thereof virtue.

There can be no friendship where there is no freedom.

Friendship loves a free air, and will not be penned up in straight and narrow inclosures. It will speak freely and act so too; and take nothing ill where no ill is meant, nay, where it is, it will easily forgive, and forget too, upon small acknowledgments.

Friends are true twins in soul; they sympathize in everything, and have the same love and aversion. One is not happy without the other; nor can either of them be miserable alone. As if they could change bodies they take their turns in pain as well as in pleasure; relieving one another in their most adverse conditions. What one enjoys the other cannot want.

A true friend unbosoms freely, advises justly, assists readily, adventures boldly, takes all patiently, defends courageously, and continues a friend unchangeably.

60

T HE KINGDOM OF GOD COM-
eth not with outward show. Neither shall men saye, Lo,
here! or lo, there! for behold, the kingdom of God is
within you.

Gather not treasure on
earth, where rust and moth do corrupte, and where
theves breake through and steale; but gather ye treasure in heaven, where rust and moth corrupte not, nor
theves breake through. For where your treasure is,
there will your heart be also. The light of the body is
the eye; if therefore thine eye be single, thy whole body
shall be full of light. But if thine eye be wycked, thy
whole body shall be full of darkness. If therefore the
light that is in thee be darkness, how great is that
darkness!

No man can serve two mas-
ters: for either he will hate the one and love the other;
or else he will hold to the one and despise the other.
Ye cannot serve God and mammon. Therefore I say
unto you, Be not careful for your lyfe, what ye shall
eate or what ye shall drinke; nor yet for your body,
what rayment ye shall weare. Is not the lyfe more than
meate, and the body than rayment?

Consider the lilies of the field, how they grow; they toil not, neither do they spin; and yet I say unto you, that even Solomon in all his glory was not arrayed like one of these. Therefore take no thought, saying What shall we eate? or, What shall we drinke? or, Wherewith shall we be clothed? But seke ye rather the kingdom of God and the right-wisnesse* thereof, and all these things shall be added unto you. Be not anxious for the morrow; for the morrow shall be anxious for the things of itself. Sufficient unto eche day is the trouble thereof.

61

HE WHO BINDS TO HIMSELF A JOY
Does the wingèd life destroy;
But he who kisses the joy as it flies
Lives in eternity's sun rise.

62

Those for whom the world smells only of matter, smell themselves only; those that see nothing but passing phenomena, see themselves and no deeper. Not in contemplation of the stars that wheel across the sky shall we discover Thee, O God, Thou who didst enrich with madness Don Quixote! The discovery comes by watching, from the depths of our hearts, the soaring of love's aspirations.

63

K EEP THYSELF TO THE
first naked apprehensions of things as they present
themselves to thee, and add not unto them. Is it reported that such a one speaketh ill of thee? Very well:
that he speaketh ill of thee, so much is reported. But
that thou art hurt thereby is not reported: that were
the addition of opinion, which thou must exclude. I
see that my child is sick? That he is sick, I see; but
that he is in danger of his life therefrom, I see it not.
So must thou habitually keep thyself to the first motions and apprehensions of things, being vigilant that
thou add nothing of mere opinion from within thyself. Should one say, then: This day have I come out
of all my trouble? Nay, it should rather be: This day
have I cast out my trouble. For that which troubled
thee, whatever it may have been, was not outside thee,
but within, in thine own opinion, whence, before thou
canst be truly and constantly at ease, it must be cast
out.

64

B<small>UT COM THOU GODDESS FAIR AND FREE,</small>
In Heav'n ycleap'd Euphrosyne,
And, by men, heart-easing Mirth—

Haste thee nymph, and bring with thee
Jest and youthful Jollity,
Quips and Cranks and wanton Wiles,
Nods and Becks, and wreathèd Smiles
Such as hang on Hebe's cheek
And love to live in dimple sleek;
Sport that wrinkled Care derides,
And Laughter holding both his sides.

Com, and trip it as ye go
On the light fantastick toe,
And in thy right hand lead with thee
The Mountain Nymph sweet Liberty;
And if I give thee honour due,
Mirth, admit me of thy crue
To live with her, and live with thee,
In unreprovèd pleasures free.

65

ALL WHATEVER IS SPOKEN, written, or taught of God, without the knowledge of the signature, is dumb and void of understanding; for it proceeds only from an historical conjecture, from the mouth of another, wherein the spirit without knowledge is dumb; but if the spirit opens to him the *signature,* then he understands the speech of another; and further, he understands how the spirit has manifested and revealed itself (out of the essence through the principle) in the sound with the voice. For though I see one to speak, teach, preach, and write of God, and though I hear and read the same, yet this is not sufficient for me to understand him; but if his sound and spirit out of his signature and similitude enter into my own similitude, and imprint his similitude into mine, then I may understand him really and fundamentally, be it either spoken or written, if he has the hammer that can strike my bell.

By this we know, that all human properties proceed from one; that they all have but one only root and mother; otherwise one man could not understand another in the sound, for with the sound or speech the form notes and imprints itself into the similitude of another; a like tone or sound catches and moves another, and in the sound the spirit imprints its own similitude, which it has conceived in the essence, and brought to form in the principle.

The signature or form is no spirit, but the receptacle, container, or cabinet of the spirit, wherein it lies; for the signature stands in the essence, and is as a lute that lieth still, and is indeed a dumb thing that is neither heard nor understood; but if it be played upon, then its form is understood, in what form and tune it stands, and according to what note it is set. Thus likewise the signature of nature in its form is a dumb essence: it is as a prepared instrument of music, upon which the will's spirit plays; what strings he touches, they sound according to their property . . . and man wants nothing but the wise master that can strike his instrument, which is the true spirit of the high might of eternity.

66

I MADE A POSIE, WHILE THE DAY RAN BY:
Here will I smell my remnant out, and tie
    My life within this band.
But time did becken to the flowers, and they
By noon most cunningly did steal away,
    And wither'd in my hand.

Farewell deare flowers, sweetly your time ye spent,
Fit, while ye liv'd, for smell or ornament,
    And after death for cures.
I follow straight without complaints or grief,
Since, if my scent be good, I care not if
    It be as short as yours.

67

Drive your cart and your plow over the bones of the dead.

He who desires but acts not, breeds pestilence.

A fool sees not the same tree that a wise man sees.

The hours of folly are measur'd by the clock; but of wisdom, no clock can measure.

All wholesome food is caught without a net or a trap.

The most sublime act is to set another before you.

The pride of the peacock is the glory of God. The lust of the goat is the bounty of God. The wrath of the lion is the wisdom of God. The nakedness of woman is the work of God.

What is now proved was once only imagin'd.

The cistern contains: the fountain overflows.

One thought fills immensity.

The soul of sweet delight
can never be defil'd.

To create a little flower is
the labour of ages.

Sooner murder an infant
in its cradle than nurse unacted desires.

Truth can never be told so
as to be understood, and not be believed.

Everything that lives is
holy .

68

BETIMES IN THE MORNING
say to thyself, This day I shall have to do with an idle
curious man, with an unthankful man, a railer, a
crafty, false, or an envious man. All these ill qualities
have happened unto them through ignorance of that
which is truly good and truly bad. But I that understand the nature of that which is good, that it alone is
to be desired, and of that which is bad, that it alone is
truly odious and shameful: who know moreover that
this transgressor, whosoever he be, is my kinsman, not
by the same blood and seed, but by participation of
the same reason and of the same divine particle; how
can I either be hurt by any of those, since it is not in
their power to make me incur anything that is truly
reproachful? or angry, and ill affected towards him
who by nature is so near unto me? for we are all born
to be fellow workers, as the feet, the hands, and the
eyelids, as the rows of the upper and under teeth: for
such therefore to be in opposition is against nature.

69

L‍OVE INDEED IS A LIGHT burden, not cumbering but lightening the bearer; and maketh glad both young and old. Love is ghostly wine freshening and fortifying the minds of its chosen, and raising them beyond thought or care of worldly allurements. By holy love no lover can lose aught, but needs must gain much if he keep it truly in heart. Love without pain lives in the lover's soul; for love makes perfect, but pain mortifies.

Love is the fairest and most profitable guest that a reasonable creature can entertain. To God it is the most acceptable and pleasing of all things. Not only does it comfort the spirit with sweetness and wisdom, and make her one with God, but it doth so constrain flesh and blood that a man slip never into the snare of trivial beguilements. In the light and warmth of love our life grows strong and comely: a better dwelling, nor a sweeter, never I found.

70

ART THOU POOR, YET HAST THOU GOLDEN SLUMBERS?
    O sweet content!
  Art thou rich, yet is thy mind perplexed?
    O punishment!
  Dost thou laugh to see how fools are vexed
To add to golden numbers golden numbers?
      O sweet content! O sweet, O sweet content!

Work apace, apace, apace, apace:
Honest labour bears a lovely face.

71

A

CTING WITHOUT DESIGN,
occupying oneself without making a business of it,
finding the great in what is small and the many in the
few, repaying injury with kindness, effecting difficult
things while they are easy, and managing great things
in their beginnings: this is the method of Tao.★ All
difficult things have their origin in that which is easy,
and great things in that which is small.

The wise man does not lay
up treasure. The more he gives to others, the more he
has for his own. This is the Tao of Heaven, which pene-
trates but does not injure. This is the Tao of the wise
man, who acts but does not strive.

Whoso bendeth himself
shall be straightened. Whoso emptieth himself shall
be filled. Whoso weareth himself away shall be re-
newed. Whoso humbleth himself shall be exalted.
Whoso exalteth himself shall be abased. Therefore
doth the Sage cling to simplicity.

Tao is without limitation;
its depth is the source of whatsoever is. It makes sharp
things round, it brings order out of chaos, it obscures
the brilliant, it is wholly without attachment. I know

not who gave it birth; it is more ancient than God.

The Tao that is the subject of discussion is not the true Tao. The quality which can be named is not its true attribute.

72

Ye have herde how it is sayd, An eye for an eye, a tooth for a tooth. But I saye unto you, that ye withstand not wrong; but if a man give thee a blow on thy right cheke, tourne to him the other; and if any man will sue thee at the lawe, and take thy coat from thee, lett him have thy clooke also; and whosoever will compell thee to goo a mile, goo with him twain. Give to him that axeth, and from him that wolde borrow tourne not awaye.

Ye have herde how it is sayde, Thou shalt love thy neighbour, and hate thine enemy. But I saye unto you, Love your enemies, blesse them that curse you, do good to them that hate you, and pray for them that despitefully use you, and persecute you; that ye may be the [true] children of your heavenly Father: for he maketh his sunne to arise on the evill and on the good, and sendeth his reyne on the juste and on the unjuste. For if ye shall love them which love you, what rewarde shall ye have? Doo not the taxgatherers even so? And if ye be friendly to your brethren only, what singular thing doo ye? Doo not the taxgatherers likewise? Be ye therefore perfect [in love], even as your heavenly Father is perfect.

73

When Abraham sat at his tent door, according to his custom, waiting to entertain strangers, he espied an old man, stooping and leaning on his staff, weary with age and travail, coming towards him, who was a hundred years of age; he received him kindly, washed his feet, provided supper, caused him to sit down; but, observing that the old man ate and prayed not, nor begged a blessing on his meat, he asked him why he did not worship the God of heaven. The old man told him that he worshipped the fire only, and acknowledged no other God. At which answer Abraham grew so zealously angry, that he threw the old man out of his tent, and exposed him to all the evils of the night and an unguarded condition. When the old man was gone, God called to Abraham, and asked him where the stranger was. He replied, 'I thrust him away, because he did not worship thee'. God answered him, 'I have suffered him these hundred years, though he dishonoured me; and wouldst thou not endure him one night, when he gave thee no trouble?'

74

LOVE BADE ME WELCOME: YET MY SOUL DREW BACK,
    Guiltie of dust and sinne.
But quick-ey'd Love, observing me grow slack
    From my first entrance in,
Drew nearer to me, sweetly questioning
    If I lack'd anything.

'A guest,' I answer'd, 'worthy to be here.'
    Love said, 'You shall be he.'
'I the unkinde, ungratefull? Ah my deare
    I cannot look on thee.'
Love took my hand and smiling did reply,
    'Who made the eyes but I?'

'Truth, Lord; but I have marr'd them: let my shame
    Go where it doth deserve.'
'And know you not,' sayes Love, 'who bore the blame?'
    'My deare, then will I serve.'
'You must sit down,' sayes Love, 'and taste my meat.'
    So I did sit and eat.

75

I AM SOMETIMES BLAMED for not labouring more earnestly to bring down the good of which I prate into the lives of other men. My critics suppose, apparently, that I mean by the good some particular way of life or some type of character which is alone virtuous, and which ought to be propagated. Alas, their propagandas! How they have filled this world with hatred, darkness, and blood! How they are still the eternal obstacle, in every home and in every heart, to a simple happiness! I have no wish to propagate any particular character, least of all my own; my conceit does not take that form. I wish individuals, and races, and nations to be themselves, and to multiply the forms of perfection and happiness, as nature prompts them. The only thing which I think might be propagated without injustice to the types thereby suppressed is harmony; enough harmony to prevent the interference of one type with another, and to allow the perfect development of each type. The good, as I can conceive it, is happiness, happiness for each man after his own heart, and for each hour according to its inspiration.

76

Y<small>E HUMBLE AND GENTLE</small> in your conversation; and of few words, I charge you; but always pertinent when you speak; hearing out before you attempt to answer; and then speaking as if you would persuade, not impose.

In making friends consider well first; and when you are fixed, be true; not wavering by reports, nor deserting in affliction; for that becomes not the good and virtuous.

Be no busybodies: meddle not with other folks' matter but when in conscience and duty prest; for it procures trouble and ill-manners, and is very unseemly to wise men.

77

I SAW THAT THE WAY TO become rich and blessed was . . . to approach more near, or to see more clearly with the eye of our understanding, the beauties and glories of the whole world: and to have communion with the Deity in the riches of God and Nature. I saw moreover that it did not so much concern us what objects were before us, as with what eyes we beheld them, with what affections we esteemed them, and what apprehensions we had about them. All men see the same objects, but do not equally understand them. Intelligence is the tongue that discerns and tastes them, Knowledge is the Light of Heaven, Love is the Wisdom and Glory of God, Life extended to all objects is the sense that enjoys them. So that Knowledge, Life, and Love are the very means of all enjoyment, which above all things we must seek for and labour after. All objects are in God Eternal: which we by perfecting our faculties are made to enjoy. Which then are turned into Act, when they are exercised about their objects; but without them are desolate and idle; or discontented and forlorn. Whereby I perceived the meaning of the definition wherein Aristotle describeth Felicity, when he saith, Felicity is the perfect virtue in a perfect Life. For that life is perfect when it is perfectly extended to all objects, and perfectly sees them, and perfectly loves them: which is done by a perfect exercise of virtue about them.

78

By the accident of good fortune a man may rule the world for a time. But by virtue of love he may rule the world for ever.

79

___

THESE EXQUISITE AND AB-
surd fancies of mine—little curiosities, and greedi-
nesses, and impulses to kiss and touch and snatch, and
all the vanities and artless desires that nest and sing
in my heart like birds in a bush—all these, we are now
told, are an inheritance from our pre-human past, and
were hatched long ago in very ancient swamps and
forests. But what of that? I like to share in the dumb
delights of birds and animals, to feel my life drawing
its sap from roots deep in the soil of Nature. I am proud
of those bright-eyed, furry, four-footed or feathered
progenitors, and not at all ashamed of my cousins, the
Tigers and Apes and Peacocks.

80

B<small>EAR ALWAYS IN MIND</small>
that it is not in you to judge anyone. No one is fitted
to pass judgment on a criminal till he realizes that he
himself is just such another, and that he, perhaps more
than all men, is himself responsible for the crime.
Say to yourself: Had I been perfect in love there might
have been no criminal standing before me to-day. If
in this fashion you can take his crime upon yourself,
freely do so, suffer in his behalf, and let him go un-
blamed. Even if the law has ordained you his judge,
act in this spirit so far as may be: then he will go away
chastened, and the love in him will condemn him more
sternly than you have done. And if it chance otherwise,
if your love fail of response in him and he go away
mocking you, do not lose heart on that account; for
that will show only that he is not yet ready for deliverance from himself. In due time he *will* be ready; and
if not, it is no matter. If not he, then another in his
stead, will by understanding and suffering learn the
way of love; and so the truth will be fulfilled. Hold fast
to this; for herein lies all the hope and faith of the
saints.

81

THEN LET WRATH REMOVE;
Love will do the deed;
              For with love
Stonie hearts will bleed.

Love is swift of foot;
Love's a man of warre,
              And can shoot,
And can hit from farre.

82

MAN DOTH NOT SEEM TO
rest satisfied, either with fruition of that wherewith
his life is preserved, or with performance of such actions as advance him most deservedly in estimation;
but doth further covet, yea oftentimes manifestly pur-
sue with great sedulity and earnestness, that which
cannot stand him in any stead for vital use; that which
exceedeth the reach of sense; yea somewhat above
capacity of reason, somewhat divine and heavenly,
which with hidden exultation it rather surmiseth than
conceiveth; somewhat it seeketh, and what that is di-
rectly it knoweth not, yet very intentive desire thereof
doth so incite it, that all other known delights and
pleasures are laid aside—they give place to the search
of this but only suspected desire.

83

THE BOUNDED IS LOATHED
by its possessor. The same dull round, even of a universe, would soon become a mill with complicated
wheels.

If any could desire what he
is incapable of possessing, despair must be his eternal
lot.

The desire of Man being
infinite, the possession is infinite and himself infinite.

He who sees the Infinite in
all things, sees God. He who sees the Ratio only, sees
himself only.

Therefore God becomes as
we are, that we may be as he is.

84

He was a strict and severe applier of all things to himself, and would first have his self-love satisfied, and then his love of all others. It is true that self-love is dishonorable, but then it is when it is alone. And self-endedness is mercenary, but then it is when it endeth in oneself. It is more glorious to love others, and more desirable, but by natural means to be attained. That pool must first be filled that shall be made to overflow. He was ten years studying before he could satisfy his self-love; and now finds nothing more easy than to love others better than oneself: and that to love mankind so is the comprehensive method to all Felicity. For it makes a man delightful to God and men, to himself and spectators, and God and men delightful to him, and all creatures infinitely in them. But as not to love oneself at all is brutish, or rather absurd and stonish (for the beasts do love themselves), so hath God by rational methods enabled us to love others better than ourselves, and thereby made us the most glorious creatures. Had we not loved ourselves at all, we could never have been obliged to love anything. So that self-love is the basis of all love. But when we do love ourselves, and self-love is satisfied infinitely in all its desires and possible demands, then it is easily led to regard the Benefactor more than itself, and for His sake overflows abundantly to all others. So that God by satisfying my self-love, hath enabled and engaged me to love others.

85

FOR BEAUTY BEING THE BEST OF ALL WE KNOW
Sums up the unsearchable and secret aims
Of nature, and on joys whose earthly names
Were never told can form and sense bestow;
And man hath sped his instinct to outgo
The step of science; and against her shames
Imagination stakes out heavenly claims,
Building a tower above the head of woe.

Nor is there fairer work for beauty found
Than that she win in nature her release
From all the woes that in the world abound:
Nay with his sorrow may his love increase,
If from man's greater need beauty redound,
And claim his tears for homage of his peace.

86

F ORCE MAY SUBDUE, BUT
Love gains; and he that forgives first wins the laurel.

To be furious in religion is
to be irreligiously religious.

There is nothing more un-
natural to religion than contentions about it.

The longest sword, the
strongest lungs, the most voices, are false measures of
truth.

It is better for us that there
should be difference of judgement, if we keep charity:
but it is most unmanly to quarrel because we differ.

Let him that is assured that
he errs in nothing, take upon him to condemn every
man that errs in anything.

If I have not a friend, God
send me an enemy, that I may hear of my faults. To
be admonished of an enemy is next to having a friend.

Reason is not a shallow
thing: it is the first participation from God; therefore,
he that observes reason observes God.

The reason of our mind is
the best instrument we have to work withal.

He that is light of belief
will be as light of unbelief if he has a mind to it; by
the same reason, he will as easily believe an error as a
truth, and as easily disbelieve a truth as an error.

87

Recognizing my own inner consciousness, the psyche, so clearly, I cannot understand time. It is eternity now. I am in the midst of it. It is about me in the sunshine; I am in it, as the butterfly in the light-laden air. Nothing has to come; it is now. Now is eternity; now is the immortal life.

88

ONE OF THE MOST SUB-
lime moments in literature occurs in that scene between Raskolnikoff, the neurotic student, and the girl
Sonia, who lives and supports her mother and the
younger children by selling the pleasure of her body
to casual purchasers. Raskolnikoff (who is not one of
these latter, but a friend of the family) talks with brutal
directness of her future, reminding her that her mother
is in the last stage of consumption and must soon die.
'And your little sister,' he says brusquely, 'it will be
the same trade for her one day, I suppose?' 'Ah no!'
cries Sonia: 'God would never permit such a thing.'
Whereupon Raskolnikoff distresses her anew by questioning the value of her God. There is silence. He
paces up and down the room in gloomy agitation. At
last he approaches her, rests his two hands on her
drooping shoulders, and gazes angrily into her face.
But suddenly he kneels before her and kisses her feet.
She shrinks back in fear, thinking him crazy. 'What
are you doing? And to *me*?' 'To you?' he answers, ris-
ing. 'No, not to you. I salute, in your person, all suffering humanity.'

89

H AD THINE ART NOT SKILL TO CHANGE
Dream into a deed of sense?
Did the baffled heart recoil
On itself in penitence?

When thy lovely sin has been
Wasted in a long despair,
World-forgetting, it may look
Upon thee with an angel air.

There was never sin of thine
But within its heart did dwell
A beauty that could whisper thee
Of the high heaven from which it fell.

90

We are in the world
like men playing at Tables; the chance is not in our
power; but to play it, is; and when it is fallen we must
manage it as we can and let nothing trouble us but
when we doe a base action, or speak like a fool, or think
wickedly: these things God hath put into our powers:
but concerning those things which are wholly in the
choice of another, they cannot fall under our delibera-
tion, and therefore neither are they fit for our passions.
My fear may make me miserable but it cannot prevent
what another hath in his power and purpose: and
prosperities can only be enjoyed by them who fear
not at all to lose them, since the amazement and passion concerning the future takes off all the pleasure of
the present possession. Therefore if thou hast lost thy
land, doe not also lose thy constancy: and if thou must
die a little sooner, yet doe not die impatiently. For no
chance is evil to him that is content, and to a man nothing is miserable unless it be unreasonable. No man
can make another man to be his slave, unless he hath
first enslaved himself to life and death, to pleasure or
pain, to hope or fear. Command these passions, and
you are freer than the Parthian Kings.

91

M EN ARE DISTURBED, NOT
by things, but by the notions they form concerning
things. Death, for example, is not in itself terrible; for
it did not appear so to Socrates; the terror resides
only in our opinion. When therefore we are hindered,
or disturbed, or grieved, let us seek the cause rather
in ourselves than elsewhere. It is the action of an un-
instructed person to lay the fault of his own bad condition upon others; of a partly instructed person, to
lay the fault on himself; and of one perfectly instructed, neither on others, nor on himself.

92

THE WORST PART OF THIS
vanity is its unteachableness. Tell it anything, and it
has known it long ago; and outruns information and
instruction, or else proudly puffs at it.

Whereas the greatest un-
derstandings doubt most, are readiest to learn, and
least pleased with themselves; this, with nobody else.

For though they stand on
higher ground, and so see farther than their neighbours, they are yet humbled by their prospect, since
it shows them something so much higher, and above
their reach.

And truly then it is that
sense shines with the greatest beauty, when it is set in
humility.

93

Y<small>OU NEVER ENJOY THE</small>
world aright, till the Sea itself floweth in your veins,
till you are clothed with the heavens, and crowned
with the stars: and perceive yourself to be the sole
heir of the whole world, and more than so, because men
are in it who are every one sole heirs as well as you.
Till you can sing and rejoice and delight in God, as
misers do in gold, and Kings in sceptres, you never
enjoy the world. Till your spirit filleth the whole
world, and the stars are your jewels; till you are as
familiar with the ways of God in all Ages as with your
walk and table: till you are intimately acquainted with
that shady nothing out of which the world was made:
till you love men so as to desire their happiness, with
the thirst equal to the zeal of your own; till you delight in God for being good to all: you never enjoy the
world. Till you more feel it than your private estate,
and are more present in the hemisphere, considering
the glories and the beauties there, than in your own
house: Till you remember how lately you were made,
and how wonderful it was when you came into it: and
more rejoice in the palace of your glory, than if it had
been made but to-day morning.

Yet further, you never enjoy the world aright, till you so love the beauty of enjoying it, that you are covetous and earnest to persuade others to enjoy it. And so perfectly hate the abominable corruption of men in despising it, that you had rather suffer the flames of Hell than willingly be guilty of their error. There is so much blindness and ingratitude and damned folly in it. The world is a mirror of infinite beauty, yet no man sees it. It is a Temple of Majesty, yet no man regards it. It is a region of Light and Peace, did not men disquiet it. It is the Paradise of God.

94

I SEE MYSELF IN LIFE AS A
part of a great physical being that strains and I believe
grows towards beauty, and of a great mental being
that strains and I believe grows towards knowledge
and power. In this persuasion that I am a gatherer of
experience, a mere tentacle that arranges thought beside thought for this being of the species, this being
that grows beautiful and powerful, in this persuasion
I find the ruling idea of which I stand in need, the ruling idea that reconciles and adjudicates among my
warring motives. In it I find both concentration of
myself and escape from myself; in a word, I find Salvation.

95

IN THE RAPT SILENCE OF THE GREEN MIDNIGHT,
  Dead, save that in the height
Stars moved; still, save that fell
Timid lisp of leaves that awake and shiver;
The eternal lapse of time, grown audible,
Rose up into my hearing like a knell,
Exhaustless, large, sustained; and in that river
I knew myself grey driftwood rolled along
    In loneliness forever.

    But it was not for long,
For soon Love's knowledge like a golden gong
Rang flaming through my spirit, and time was naught,
And life and death, earth and the stars were caught
Suddenly into a holocaust of song.

    We who alone are wise
Seeing we have the sign to exorcize
This ghost of desolation, let us tend
    Love's fire until the end . . .

Let us be patient, tender, wise, forgiving,
    In this strange task of living;

For if we fail each other, each will be
Grey driftwood lapsing to the bitter sea.

96

REMEMBER, NOT HE WHO gives ill-language, or a blow, affronts; but the fancy that conceives these things as affronting. Therefore when anyone seems to provoke you, be assured that it is your own opinion only that provokes you. Try, then, not to be hurried by appearance into a false opinion; for if you once gain time and respite you will the more easily command yourself.

If a person had delivered up your body to anyone whom he met in his way, you would feel shame. And do you feel no shame in delivering up your own mind to be disconcerted and confounded by anyone who chances to give you ill-language?

97

Have a care of resentment, or taking things amiss; a natural, ready, and most dangerous passion: but be apter to remit than to resent: it is more Christian and wise. For a softness often conquers where rough opposition fortifies, so resentment, seldom having any bounds, makes many times greater fault than it finds: for some people have outresented their wrong so far, that they made themselves faultier by it; by which they cancel the debt through a boundless passion, overthrow their interest and advantage, and become debtor to the offender.

98

LET ME NOT TO THE MARRIAGE OF TRUE MINDES
Admit impediments: love is not love
Which alters when it alteration findes,
Or bends with the remover to remove;
O no, it is an ever fixed marke
That looks on tempests and is never shaken;
It is the star to every wandring barke,
Whose worths unknowne, although his higth be taken.
Love's not Times foole, though rosie lips and cheeks
Within his bending sickles compasse come;
Love alters not with his breefe houres and weekes,
But beares it out even to the edge of doome:
   If this be error and upon me proved,
   I never writ, nor no man ever loved.

99

ALL SPEECH IS A HAZARD; oftener than not it is the most hazardous kind of deed. It is a fateful thing to administer the sacrament of the word to those destined not to understand the real significance of what we say. No faith in the spirit is too robust for us when we address the slow-witted, trusting them to understand us without understanding, and confident that the seed will drop, all unknown to them, in the furrows of their souls.

100

If it be asked, what is a godlike man, a partaker of the divine, the answer is: he that lives and shines in the divine Light, he that kindles and is consumed with the divine Love, he indeed is a citizen of Eternity, and a partaker in the being of God.

101

By HUMANITY WE SEARCH
into the powers and faculties of the Soul, enquire into
the excellencies of human nature, consider its wants,
survey its inclinations, propensities and desires, ponder
its principles, proposals, and ends, examine the causes
and fitness of all, the worth of all, the excellency of all.
Whereby we come to know what man is in this world,
what his sovereign end and happiness, and what is the
best means by which he may attain it. And by this we
come to see what wisdom is: which namely is a knowl-
ledge exercised in finding out the way to perfect happiness, by discerning man's real wants and sovereign
desires. We come moreover to know God's goodness,
in seeing into the causes wherefore He implanted such
faculties and inclinations in us, and the objects and
ends prepared for them. This leadeth us to Divinity.
For God gave man an endless intellect, to see all things,
and a proneness to covet them, because they are His
treasures; and an infinite variety of apprehensions and
affections, that he might have an all-sufficiency in himself to enjoy them; a curiosity profound and unsatiable
to stir him up to look into them: an ambition great
and everlasting to carry him to the highest honours,

thrones, and dignities: an emulation whereby he might be animated and quickened by all examples, a tenderness and compassion whereby he may be united to all persons, a sympathy and love to virtue; a tenderness of his credit in every soul, that he might delight to be honoured in all persons; an eye to behold Eternity and the Omnipresence of God, that he might see Eternity, and dwell within it; a power of admiring, loving, and prizing, that seeing the beauty and goodness of God, he might be united to it for evermore.

102

Y<small>E BLESSED CREATURES, I HAVE HEARD THE CALL</small>
    Ye to each other make; I see
The heavens laugh with you in your jubilee;
    My heart is at your festival,
    My head hath its coronal,
The fullness of your bliss, I feel—I feel it all.
    O evil day! if I were sullen
    While Earth herself is adorning,
       This sweet May-morning,
    And the Children are culling
       On every side,
    In a thousand valleys far and wide,
    Fresh flowers . . .

103

THE GREAT SECRET OF morals is love; or a going-out of our nature, and an identification of ourselves with the beautiful which exists in thought, action, or person, not our own. A man, to be greatly good, must imagine intensely and comprehensively; he must put himself in the place of another and of many others; the pains and pleasures of his species must become his own. The great instrument of moral good is the imagination.

104

Our institutions and so-
cial customs seem all to assume a definiteness of pref-
erence, a singleness and a limitation of love, which is
not psychologically justifiable. People do not, I think,
fall naturally into agreement with these assumptions;
they train themselves to agreement. They take refuge
from experiences that seem to carry with them the risk
at least of perplexing situations, in a theory of barred
possibilities and locked doors. How far this shy and
cultivated irresponsive lovelessness towards the world
at large may not carry with it the possibility of com-
pensating intensities, I do not know. Quite equally
probable is a starvation of one's emotional nature.

The same reasons that
make me decide against mere wanton abstinences
make me hostile to the common convention of emotional indifference to most of the charming and inter-
esting people one encounters. In pleasing and being
pleased, in the mutual interest, the mutual opening
out of people to one another, is the key of the door to
all sweet and mellow living.

105

I HAVE SAID THAT THE SOUL IS NOT MORE THAN THE
body,
And I have said that the body is not more than the
soul,
And nothing, not God, is greater to one than one's
self is,
And whoever walks a furlong without sympathy walks
to his own funeral drest in his shroud,
And I or you pocketless of a dime may purchase the
pick of the earth,
And to glance with an eye or show a bean in its pod
confounds the learning of all times,
And there is no trade or employment but the young
man following it may become a hero,
And there is no object so soft but it makes a hub for
the wheel'd universe,
And I say to any man or woman, Let your soul stand
cool and composed before a million universes.

106

IF THE MISDOING OF MEN move you to indignation and overwhelm you with pain, so that you are inclined even to take vengeance on the misdoers, restrain that inclination above all things. Go rather and seek suffering for yourself, as though you yourself had been guilty of that misdoing. Accept that suffering, and endure it: so shall your heart be fortified, and you will learn to recognize wherein lies your own guilt in this matter. For you to those misdoers might have been as a light shining in darkness, even as the one man perfect in love: and in this you failed them. By that love, had you attained it, you might have illumined the way for others too. Or it may be that your light did shine before men, and that you yet cannot perceive that any have been saved by it. Have faith none the less, and doubt not the virtue of the heavenly light. Believe that if they have not been saved now they will be saved hereafter. And if they themselves should never be saved, then will their sons be, or their sons' sons; for, though you die, and the world knows you no more, the light of your love shall never be put out.

107

WHO HAS NOT FELT, THOUGH IT
 might be no more
Than shadow of a phantom at high noon,
The shuddering thought, If it were possible
This life of mine should be a soul alone,
The momentary spangle in the dark
Of its own useless littleness of light!—
This is the furthest end of misery
Life can look to; and the most blessed life
Is the most opposite: spirit which lives
Divining everywhere perceiving spirit,
The answer to itself; which as it knows
Itself experience the whole world gives,
Knows that itself is to the whole world given.
That man shall bless his life, who understands
In everything that is the living creature,
Experience that each by each is shaped
As a crag shapes the moving of the waves
About its base, and by the waves is shaped:
A universe of lives, infinite world
Of mutual structure of experience;
So to know this that in his life he dwells
The conscious image of that universe

Where each in all and all in each must live;
And loves to give the best exchange he can
For what he takes; and finds, the more he gives,
The lovelier grows the world his life receives:
Ever brighter the concourse in his soul
Of the whole kind of creatures, ever more nobly
In one majestic architecture made,
Ever more glorifying the soul that lives
Imagining all this beauty; until he says,
This is the Kingdom of God, and what am I
Who dwell in it?—Then into himself he looks,
And round the central splendor of his soul
Perceives what boundless region thence expands,
Darkening into terrible distances:
Yes, and far off, ghosts of abomination,
And mysteries of evil threatening him
Ten times more fearful than the world could be
Before he loved it. Dreading then himself,
Outward again he turns his mind to look
Upon his kingdom, land and sea and stars,
Flowers and beasts and men—the lovely world
Like anguish strikes its loveliness into him;
He is the beauty he sees; and suddenly knows
The two infinities that make the world—
Infinite number of spirits in their life
Of power on one another, and each spirit
Infinite substance: the kingdom and the king!
Then, feeling himself one substance with all being,
Again he looks within: and instantly
Consumes in his own soul's unthinkable
Immense of light; and for one heavenly moment,

Himself the kingdom and himself the king,
He is the glory of God and God in his glory.
The moment ends: but like perpetual dawn
He lives thereafter; the palace where he dwells,
This structure of the souls of all the world,
Instinct, like early morning air, with gleam
Of rose and beryl, hyacinth and silver,
With the continual morrow of the king
Returning to his kingdom.

108

L OOK NOT OUT, BUT WITH-
in; let not another's liberty be your snare: neither
act by imitation, but by sense and feeling of God's
power in yourselves: crush not the tender buddings
of it in your souls, nor overrun in your desires, and
warmness of affections, the holy and gentle motions
of it. Remember it is a still voice, that speaks to us in
this way; and that it is not to be heard in the noises
and hurries of the mind; but it is distinctly understood in a retired frame.

109

IN SAYING 'I KNOW WHO I am' Don Quixote said only: 'I know what I will to be'. That is the hinge of all human life: to know what one wills to be. Little ought you to care who you are; the urgent thing is what you will to be. The being that you are is but an unstable, perishable being, which eats of the earth and which the earth some day will eat; what you will to be is the idea of you in God, the Consciousness of the universe; it is the divine idea of which you are the manifestation in time and space. And your longing impulse toward the one you will to be is only homesickness drawing you toward your divine home. Man is complete and upstanding only when he would be more than man.

110

THE WORLD GLOBES ITSELF
in a drop of dew. The microscope cannot find the
animalcule which is less perfect for being little. Eyes,
ears, taste, smell, motion, resistance, appetite, and
organs of reproduction that take hold on eternity—
all find room to consist in the small creature. So do
we put our life into every act. The true doctrine of
omnipresence is, that God reappears with all his parts
in every moss and cobweb. The value of the universe
contrives to throw itself into every point. If the good
is there, so is the evil; if the affinity, so the repulsion;
if the force, so the limitation. Thus is the universe
alive.

111

Religion is not a hear-say, a presumption, a supposition; is not a customary pretension and profession; is not an affectation of any mode; is not a piety of particular fancy, consisting of some pathetic devotions, vehement expressions, bodily severities, affected anomalies, and aversions from the innocent usages of others; but consisteth in a profound humility, and a universal charity.

112

I BELIEVE ALL MANNER OF asceticism to be the vilest blasphemy—blasphemy towards the whole of the human race. I believe in the flesh and the body, which is worthy of worship—to see a perfect human body unveiled causes a sense of worship. The ascetics are the only persons who are impure. Increase of physical beauty is attended by increase of soul beauty. The soul is the higher even by gazing on beauty. Let me be fleshly perfect.

113

To him who has never realized how, by a reasonable and voluntary self-discipline, his energy may be conserved, his sensibilities quickened, and his potential of happiness increased, some measure of restraint may be safely commended. But the danger threatening the more conscientious part of mankind is that of self-suppression (and consequent impoverishment of life) in the service of false gods. Without spontaneity man's life is mechanical and unmeaning, and his morality a dead letter. Moreover, it is idle to suppose, as so many appear to do, that kindness to others is advanced by cruelty to oneself: experience, indeed, points in quite the opposite direction. Self-sacrifice has neither spiritual beauty nor any other human value if it is not, at the same time, genuine self-expression. An act of 'unselfishness' profits a man nothing, and does more harm than good, unless he is able to put his deepest self into it.

114

A s twixt two equal armies fate
  Suspends uncertain victory,
Our souls, which to advance their state
  Were gone out, hung twixt her and me.
And whilst our souls negotiate there
  We like sepulchral statues lay;
All day the same our postures were,
  And we said nothing, all the day.

If any, so by love refin'd
  That he soul's language understood
And by good love were grown all mind,
  Within convenient distance stood,
He (though he knew not which soul spake,
  Because both meant, both spake the same)
Might thence a new concoction take,
  And part far purer than he came.

This Extasy doth unperplex
  (We said) and tell us what we love.
We see by this, it was not sex;
  We see we saw not what did move.
But, as all several souls contain

Mixture of things, they know not what,
Love these mixt souls doth mix again
　And makes both one, each this and that.

A single violet transplant—
　The strength, the colour, and the size
(All which before was poor and scant)
　Redoubles still, and multiplies.
When love, with one another, so
　Interinanimates two souls,
That abler soul which thence doth flow
　Defects of loneliness controls.

We then, who are this new soul, know
　Of what we are compos'd and made;
For th' Atomies of which we grow
　Are souls whom no change can invade.
But O alas, so long, so far,
　Our bodies why do we forbear?
They are ours though they are not we: we are
　The intelligences, they the sphere.

We own them thanks because they thus
　Did us to us at first convey;
Yielded their forces, sense, to us,
　Nor are dross to us, but allay.
On man heaven's influence works not so
　But that it first imprints the air:
So soul into the soul may flow,
　Though it to body first repair.

As our blood labours to beget
　　Spirits as like souls as it can,
Because such fingers need to knit
　　That subtle knot which makes us man:
So must pure lovers' souls descend
　　To affections, and to faculties
Which sense may reach and apprehend
　　—Else a great Prince in prison lies.

To our bodies turn we then, that so
　　Weak men on love reveal'd may look;
Love's mysteries in souls doth grow,
　　But yet the body is his book.
And if some lover, such as we,
　　Have heard this dialogue of one,
Let him still mark us, he shall see
　　Small change, when we are to bodies gone.

115

THE BODIES OF LOVERS ARE THE FORMS OF
    ineffable Desire,
Male and female serpents of the Holy Spirit
Breathing out its essence in individual outline.
For the Holy Spirit is single and particular,
It is not a fire but a Shape of Fire,
It is not holiness but this Holy One—
Thou, angelic Bride or Bridegroom,
Whom my soul loves!

116

LOVE SILENCE, EVEN IN THE
mind; for thoughts are to that, as words are to the
body, troublesome: much speaking, as much thinking,
spends. True silence is the rest of the mind; and it is
to the spirit, what sleep is to the body, nourishment
and refreshment.

117

GIVE ME LIFE STRONG AND full as the brimming ocean; give me thoughts wide as its plain; give me a soul beyond these. Sweet is the bitter sea by the shore where the faint blue pebbles are lapped by the green-grey wave, where the wind-quivering foam is loth to leave the lashed stone. Sweet is the bitter sea, and the clear green in which the gaze seeks the soul, looking through the glass into itself. The sea thinks for me as I listen and ponder; the sea thinks, and every boom of the wave repeats my prayer.

118

THE STATE OF DEATH IS one of two things: either it is the absence of all being and sensation, or—and this is the common belief—it is the translation of the soul into another place. And if death be the absence of all sensation, like a sleep untroubled by any dream, it will be a wonderful gain. For if, having called to mind one night of perfect sleep, a man were asked how many days and nights of his life he had spent more agreeably than that night, I think that anyone—even the great King of Persia himself—would find them easy to count. If that be the nature of death, I for one count it a gain; for eternity must then be, in effect, no more than a single night. But if death be a journey to another place, in which, as the common belief has it, dwell all who have died, what prospect, my judges, could be more heartening than this? Would not that journey be worth taking, at the end of which, in another world, we should find ourselves rid of the self-styled judges who are here, and confronted by the true judges, who are said to sit in judgment below, such as Minos, and Rhadamanthus, and Æacus, and Triptolemus, and the other demi-gods who were just in their lives? And what

would you not give to talk with Orpheus and Musaeus
and Hesiod and Homer? If this conjecture be true, I
am willing to die many times.

119

I SPOKE OF THE WORLD
And the world replied:
Softly, softly! Till you have died
You cannot lie still. And I awoke
For that one instant—saw the grass
Clear as in transparent glass
But, long before my mind could leap
Out of its sepulchre of sleep,
The Joy, its wings and brightness, all
Had turned to grass,
        And the world replied:
Softly, softly! Till you have died
You cannot lie still. And I forgot
Whether the Joy was pain or not.

        What shall lie still?

        When I am dead—
Limbless, lifeless, feather-sped—
Goes not forth some spirit of sense
To watch and await the arising fire?
To add my still unspent desire,
To burn the excess of joy like oil,

To wave in flower, and grow in toil?
The Vision unnamed but not unseen
Promised such life . . .
    And the world replied:
Softly, softly! Till you have died
You cannot be sure. And I forgot
Whether the grass had changed or not.

120

For him who has faith, death, so far as it is his own death, ceases to possess any quality of terror. The experiment will be over, the rinsed beaker returned to its shelf, the crystals gone dissolving down the waste-pipe; the duster sweeps the bench.

121

IN NATURE EVERYTHING
has a meaning. And everything is forgiven. And it
would be strange not to forgive.

LOVE AND DO WHAT THOU WILT
WHATEVER THOU DOEST DO WITH LOVE
LET THE ROOT OF LOVE BE WITHIN
AND ONLY GOOD CAN FLOWER THEREFROM

INDEX AND NOTES

KEY TO THE INDEX

AUTHORS' NAMES ARE GIVEN, NOT ALWAYS IN FULL, BUT IN THE FORM usual in ordinary conversation. Thus Shelley is Shelley; and Rabelais, Rabelais; whereas Traherne, less generally known, is at his first entry Thomas Traherne, and thereafter Traherne simply. Where it has seemed desirable to supply fuller textual or biographical information, or where the editor has wished to indulge in the luxury of personal comment, a note has been written bearing the number of the entry to which it refers. These notes, which the reader may at his pleasure consult or neglect, occupy the section immediately following the INDEX, and their existence is signalized in the INDEX by a star. One or two more urgent notes are also indicated in the text itself, by a star placed above the particular word to which it refers. 'Tr.' stands for *translated by;* and 'revised', following the translator's name, indicates that some of his sentences have been revised by the editor, generally after consultation either with the original or (more often) with other translations. Where a translation is not otherwise ascribed, the editor is himself responsible for the form of the English version. The word 'assembled' is used to show that some few phrases or sentences have been omitted, so that what reads as a continuous passage does not so appear in the original: these liberties have been taken solely in the interest of economy, and with a scrupulous regard for the author's intention. The phrase 'conjoined passages' may be read as a more emphatic indication of the same selective process. Words and phrases that appear in the text between square brackets are editorial insertions.

INDEX

1. THOMAS TRAHERNE (1663-1674). From *Centuries of Meditations,*
   a book of which the unpublished MS was first brought to light,
   in 1908, by the late Bertram Dobell, whose modernized text is
   here used.

2. RABELAIS. Tr. Urquhart. The phrase in parenthesis is trans-
   posed in order to avoid a superficial ambiguity.

3. ST. PAUL. 1 *Corinthians.* In italicizing three pronouns I follow
   Sir Arthur Quiller-Couch (see the *Oxford Book of English
   Prose*).

4. BLAKE. From *The Marriage of Heaven and Hell.* For my Blake
   passages I have searched the invaluable Nonesuch edition (ed.
   by Geoffrey Keynes). But I have modernized the spelling and
   punctuation where it has seemed desirable to do so.

5. From Drs. Grenfell and Hunt's translation of Greek papyri discovered on the site of Oxyrhynchus, one of the chief cities of
   ancient Egypt. The first paragraph is from *Fragment of a Lost
   Gospel,* the second and third from *New Sayings of Jesus* (discovered in 1903), and the fourth from the *Logia* (discovered in
   1897). I have slightly shifted the balance of one or two sentences.
   The three fragments (in one volume) were published for the
   Egypt Exploration Fund, in 1904, by the Oxford University Press,
   with commentary and notes by the translators.

6. WILLIAM PENN. From *Fruits of Solitude.*

7. JAMES NAYLER. Believed to be his last public utterance, delivered from his deathbed. I omit: 'It never rejoyceth but through
   Sufferings; for with the World's Joy it is murthered'. And I read:

[157]

'it takes its Kingdom with Intreaty' instead of: 'and takes . . .
For biography see note ★7.

8. BLAKE. From *The Marriage of Heaven and Hell*.

9. ST. JOHN. *The First Epistle*. Conjoined passages.

10. SIEGFRIED SASSOON. From *The Heart's Journey*. Harper.

11. TRAHERNE. From *Centuries of Meditations*. Scribner.

12. MIGUEL DE UNAMUNO. From *The Life of Don Quixote and Sancho*. Tr. Homer P. Earle. Knopf.

13. BLAKE. From *Auguries of Innocence*. Assembled.

14. JEREMY TAYLOR. From *A Discourse of the Nature and Offices of Friendship*, 1657.

15. GEORGE SANTAYANA. From *Platonism and the Spiritual Life*. Scribner.

16. TRAHERNE. From *Centuries of Meditations*. Scribner.

17. BLAKE. 'The Sunflower'. I insert a comma after 'Youth', so that 'pined' may be at once recognized for what it is, a participle. This comma is not grammatically justified, since 'pined away with desire' is a defining clause; but its absence (especially when the line ends with a comma) tends to obscure the meaning, if only for a moment. For the sake of consistency I also enclose 'shrouded in snow' between commas, though with some misgiving.

18. Editor. From *Dreaming*. Revised. Harper. The sentence between quotation marks is from Joseph Conrad.

19. DOSTOEVSKY. From Father Zossima's discourse in *The Brothers Karamazov*. Freely rendered.

20. From *The Book of Wisdom*. Authorized Version. Assembled.

21. FRANCIS BACON. *On Superstition*.

22. WORDSWORTH. From *Intimations of Immortality*.

23. EMERSON. From 'The Over-Soul'.

24. NIETZSCHE. From *Also sprach Zarathustra*, published by Alfred Kröner, Leipzig. English version based on an exact translation kindly made for me by Ruth Niven.

25. RICHARD CHURCH. 'In April': from *The Glance Backward*. Dent: London.

26. MARCUS AURELIUS. From *Meditations*. Conjoined passages. My version is based on Casaubon's. It is important to remember that these admonitions were all addressed by their author to himself. In this he is the great exemplar of moralists.

27. HARRY ROBERTS. In a letter to *The New Statesman and Nation*, 29 August, 1931. See note ★27.

28. From *The Gospel according to St. John*. A blend of three translations: Tyndale, Authorized Version, and Revised Version.

29. BLAKE. Prefatory note to 'The Everlasting Gospel'.

30. RABELAIS. Tr. Urquhart. Gargantua's speech to the vanquished.

31. Based on the opening of the Fourth Gospel.

32. JEREMY TAYLOR. *Sermons*.

33. RICHARD JEFFERIES. From *The Story of My Heart*. Dutton.

34. GEORGE SANTAYANA. From *Platonism and the Spiritual Life*. Scribner.

35. PENN. From *Fruits of Solitude*.

36. FRANK KENDON. Part of poem. From unpublished MS.

37. CONFUCIUS (attributed). From *The Sayings of Confucius*: a translation of the Confucian Analects by Lionel Giles, D.Litt. Dutton. See note ★37.

38. Editor. In this very personal anthology, I have been glad to borrow other men's voices with which to express convictions of my own. But where I have failed to find some particular part of my thought stated by another, I have resorted to the unusual expedient of writing, as best I could, the passage I was in search of. For note on 'sin', see ★38.

39. SPINOZA. *Ethics*. Tr. Hale White. Oxford.

40. BOEHME. From *Signatura Rerum*. Tr. William Law. Conjoined passages.

41. MARCUS AURELIUS. *Meditations*. Tr. Casaubon.

42. RUYSBROEK. From *Die Zierde der geistlichen Hochzeit*.

43. SIEGFRIED SASSOON. From *The Heart's Journey*. Harper.

44. BENJAMIN WHICHCOTE. *Sermons.* For Whichcote and Glanvill I am indebted to Tulloch's *Rational Theology in England in the Seventeenth Century.* They are also to be found with others of their group, in Campagnac's *The Cambridge Platonists:* a volume of selections. Oxford.

45. BOEHME. From *A Dialogue between a Scholar and his Master concerning the Supersensual Life.* Tr. William Law. Conjoined passages.

46. LASCELLES ABERCROMBIE. From 'Hymn to Love', the general prelude to *Emblems of Love.* Dodd, Mead.

47. JOSEPH GLANVILL. From *Scepsis Scientifica.*

48. GUINICELLI. 'Of Moderation and Tolerance'. From *The Early Italian Poets.* Tr. Dante Gabriel Rossetti.

49. Traditional. There is a musical setting by Sir H. Walford Davies in his *Fellowship Songbook.* The original has 'God', not 'Love'.

50. JEREMY TAYLOR. *Sermons.* One (Latin) sentence omitted.

51. WORDSWORTH. From *Intimations of Immortality.*

52. GEORGE SANTAYANA. From *Soliloquies in England.* Scribner.

53. *Book of Common Prayer.* The Second Collect, *for Peace:* Morning Prayer. And the Second Collect at Evening Prayer. See note ★53.

54. H. G. WELLS. From *First and Last Things.* Watts.

55. PLATO. From *The Republic.* Tr. J. L. Davies and D. J. Vaughan. Macmillan.

56. BLAKE. No title.

57. MARCUS AURELIUS. *Meditations.* Tr. Casaubon.

58. KEATS. The opening lines of *Endymion.*

59. PENN. From *Fruits of Solitude.*

60. ST. LUKE AND ST. MATTHEW. The first paragraph from Luke, the rest Matthew. For textual details, and comment, see note ★60.

61. BLAKE. 'Eternity'. 'He who binds to himself a joy' (instead of 'bends', the usual version) is an inspired re-reading which we owe to the writer of a recent letter to *The Times Literary Sup-*

[160]

plement. It was suggested by a scrutiny of Blake's manuscript.

62. UNAMUNO. From *The Life of Don Quixote and Sancho*. Tr. Earle. Knopf.

63. MARCUS AURELIUS. From *Meditations*. Two conjoined passages. Tr. Casauban (but revised).

64. MILTON. From *l'Allegro*.

65. BOEHME. From *Signatura Rerum*. Tr. William Law. Conjoined passages.

66. GEORGE HERBERT. Two of three stanzas entitled 'Life'.

67. BLAKE. From *The Marriage of Heaven and Hell*. Selected aphorisms.

68. MARCUS AURELIUS. *Meditations*. Tr. Casaubon. One word changed.

69. RICHARD ROLLE, the Hermit of Hampole. From the *Incendium Amoris*. A paraphrase of Richard Misyn's Middle English translation. Assembled.

70. THOMAS DEKKER. Song from a play.

71. LAO-TZE. From *The Simple Way*, a translation of the *Tao-Teh-King*. Tr. Walter Gorn Old. David McKay. For 'Tao' see note ★71.

72. ST. MATTHEW. Tyndale's version, with two A.V. phrases substituted ('despitefully use you' and 'Be ye'). Also I have printed 'tax-gatherers' in place of 'publicans'.

73. JEREMY TAYLOR. From *The Liberty of Prophesying*.

74. GEORGE HERBERT. 'Love'.

75. GEORGE SANTAYANA. From *Soliloquies in England*. Scribner.

76. PENN. Fragments from *Letters to his Wife and Children*.

77. TRAHERNE. From *Centuries of Meditations*. Scribner.

78. LAO-TZE. From *The Simple Way*, a translation of the *Tao-Teh-King*. Tr. Walter Gorn Old. David McKay.

79. LOGAN PEARSAL SMITH. 'Desires', from *Trivia*. Copyright 1917, by Doubleday, Doran & Company, Inc.

80. DOSTOEVSKY. From Father Zossima's discourse in *The Brothers*

Karamazov. Freely rendered.

81. GEORGE HERBERT. Two stanzas from 'Discipline'.

82. HOOKER. From *Ecclesiastical Politie*.

83. BLAKE. Selected from a sequence of aphorisms entitled *There is no natural religion* (second series).

84. TRAHERNE. From *Centuries of Meditations*. Scribner.

85. ROBERT BRIDGES. From 'The Growth of Love' *(The Works of Robert Bridges,* 6 vols., Oxford).

86. WILLIAM PENN AND BENJAMIN WHICHCOTE. The first two are by Penn, the rest by Whichcote.

87. RICHARD JEFFERIES. From *The Story of My Heart*. Dutton.

88. The scene here briefly summarized occurs in Dostoevsky's *Crime and Punishment.*

89. A. E. 'Ancestry' from *Vale and Other Poems*. Macmillan.

90. JEREMY TAYLOR. From *Holy Living*. The influence of Epictetus is evident.

91. EPICTETUS. Tr. Elizabeth Carter (revised). Dutton.

92. PENN. From *Fruits of Solitude.*

93. TRAHERNE. From *Centuries of Meditations*. Scribner. See note ★93.

94. H. G. WELLS. From *First and Last Things*. Watts.

95. MARTIN ARMSTRONG. From 'Body and Spirit' in *Collected Poems.* Secker: London.

96. EPICTETUS. Tr. Elizabeth Carter (revised). Dutton.

97. PENN. From *Advice to his Children.*

98. SHAKESPEARE. Sonnet CXVI. The spelling is that of the Quarto. There can be little doubt that *higth*, though printed as *height* in our standard Shakespeares, was meant to be read as *highth,* a word we find also in Milton. By virtue of the alliteration between 'worth' and 'highth', and the avoidance of the rather difficult 'height be taken', this gives us a far more euphonious line.

99. UNAMUNO. From *The Life of Don Quixote and Sancho*. Tr. Earle. Knopf.

100. From the *Theologia Germanica*. Free translation. The phrase 'Citizen of Eternity' is an interpolation of my own, but in the spirit of the original.

101. TRAHERNE. From *Centuries of Meditations*. Scribner.

102. WORDSWORTH. From *Intimations of Immortality*.

103. SHELLEY. From *The Defence of Poetry*.

104. H. G. WELLS. From *First and Last Things*. Watts.

105. WHITMAN. From *Song of Myself*.

106. DOSTOEVSKY. From Father Zossima's discourse in *The Brothers Karamazov*. Freely rendered.

107. LASCELLES ABERCROMBIE. From *The Sale of Saint Thomas*. Secker: London.

108. PENN. From *The Rise and Progress of the People called Quakers*.

109. UNAMUNO. From *The Life of Don Quixote and Sancho*. Tr. Earle. Knopf.

110. EMERSON. From 'Compensation'.

111. WHICHCOTE. *Sermons*.

112. RICHARD JEFFERIES. From *The Story of My Heart*. Dutton.

113. Editor.

114. DONNE. All but the first three stanzas of 'The Extasy'. I have ventured to modernize the spelling and punctuation of this magnificent poem (already so modern in spirit), in order that its argument may be the more readily followed. Donne's own punctuation, as given in the standard edition, is more hindrance than help to a present-day reader. The device ⌢ is to aid scansion by indicating the fusion of two words upon which the stress falls equally.

115. W. J. TURNER. From *Pursuit of Psyche*. Wishart: London.

116. PENN. From *Advice to his Children*.

117. RICHARD JEFFERIES. From *The Story of My Heart*. Dutton.

118. PLATO. From *The Apology of Socrates*.

119. FRANK KENDON. From unpublished MS.

120. H. G. WELLS. From *First and Last Things*. Watts.

121. TCHEHOV. From a fragment of MS found after his death.

NOTES

★7. JAMES NAYLER (1618-1660), once a quartermaster in Cromwell's army, was already an itinerant preacher when he fell under the personal spell of George Fox, the founder of Quakerism. Of the two men, Nayler would seem to have been at once the more complex and the more lovable. If he was weaker, he was also gentler; if he possessed less practical wisdom and was liable to lose his mental balance in a way repugnant to Fox's robust common-sense, he had yet (it would seem) the more delicate spiritual perception. He was by several years Fox's senior. The mischief-making of a woman, Martha Simmonds, engendered a bitter quarrel between these two men of genius, and though, years afterwards, they were formally reconciled, there is reason to believe that Fox remained unforgiving to the end. In Fox's nature the zeal of the prophet was admixed with something of the shrewdness of a successful politician, and he could neither tolerate a blunderer nor brook opposition. With all his courage and unworldly enthusiasm—to which the world owes not a little—he had a head for policy and a talent for leadership, and the tragic paradox of his career is that his first high purpose was finally, in some measure, defeated by his own success. Beginning as the liberator of the individual conscience, a witness for 'the Inner Light' as against bibliolatry and institutionalism, he ended as the autocrat of a sect. The story of Nayler's final and absolute submission to him leaves the defeated Nayler with all the honours of a great spiritual victory.

Nayler, indeed, is one of the most striking figures, one of the most exalted spirits, in the history of seventeenth-century England. The fatal mistake of his life was that he allowed himself to become spiritually intoxicated by the adoration of a group of adoring women disciples (Martha Simmonds the chief among them), who persuaded him to ride into Bristol in a manner closely imitative of Christ's Palm Sunday entry into Jerusalem. For this offence he narrowly escaped death at the hands of a pious Parliament, which, in its great mercy, after debating the question for eleven days, preferred that he should be set on the pillory for two hours, whipped through the streets of Westminster to the Old Exchange, and, two days after, pilloried again, branded through the tongue with a hot iron, branded on the forehead with the letter B, placed on the back of a horse with his face to the tail and whipped through the streets of Bristol, and thence committed to prison and held 'till he be released by Parliament'. This sentence was duly carried out—notable work on the part of men proud of having established 'religious liberty'. The ordeal was endured by Nayler (as an eye-witness tells us) 'with astonishing and heart-melting patience'. To us, three centuries later, the punishment seems a trifle excessive, though we ourselves continue to tolerate the official torturing of convicts (flogging with the 'cat'), and the imprisonment, as ordinary criminals, of sexually deranged persons. It is perhaps beside the point that the verdict found against Nayler was contrary to the evidence. His answers to his accusers make it plain that his intention was not 'blasphemous'. What he did, or suffered to be done, was no more than a 'sign', a piece of devotional play-acting. Not he himself, but the 'seed of God' in him, was the object of veneration. However, Cromwell's Parliament had its way with him, and he died, some three years later, soon after

[166]

his release from prison. The full story should be read in Dr. Emilia Fogelklou's book, *James Nayler: the Rebel Saint* (Benn), to which I am indebted for it.

★27. THE letter quoted was written in answer to an Anglican priest who, criticizing an article by Dr. Roberts, challenged him to say what 'advice on sex matters' he (the priest) should pour into 'young modern ears'. 'Surely', wrote Dr. Roberts, 'the rector of an East End parish should need no help from me; for I refuse to take his request ironically . . . I will enumerate what I consider the salient features of a decent and intelligent Christian attitude to the so-called problems of sex—an attitude that, were I a minister of the Church, I should feel obliged to interpret in language understandable of the people'. Then follows the passage quoted in the text.

★37. IT is remarkable, suggests Dr. Giles, in the preface to his translation, 'that Confucianism, which makes no promise of blessings to be enjoyed in this life or the next, should have succeeded without the adjunct of other supernatural elements than that of ancestor-worship. Even this was accepted by Confucius as a harmless prevailing custom rather than enjoined by him as an essential part of his doctrine. Unlike Christianity and Mahometanism, the Way preached by the Chinese sage knows neither the sanction of punishment nor the stimulus of reward in an afterlife. Even Buddhism holds out the hope of Nirvana to the pure of heart, and preaches the long torment of successive rebirths to those who fall short of perfect goodness. No great religion

The Notion of Sin

is devoid of elevated precepts, or has ever failed to mould beautiful characters to attest the presence of something good and great within it. But in every case the element of supernaturalism . . . introduces a new motive for men's actions and makes it no longer possible for virtue to be followed purely for its own sake, without thought of a hereafter. . . . Virtue resting on anything but its own basis would not have seemed to him [Confucius] virtue in the true sense at all, but simply another name for prudence, foresight, or cunning.'

In a footnote the same writer tells us:

'*Jên*, the term here translated "virtue", is perhaps the most important single word in the Analects, and the real corner-stone of Confucian ethics. Its primary meaning, in accordance with the etymology, is "humanity" in the larger sense, i.e. natural goodness of heart as shown in intercourse with one's fellow-men. Hence it is sometimes best translated "loving-kindness" or "charity" in the biblical sense, though in many cases a more convenient, if vaguer, rendering is "virtue", "moral virtue", or even, as in Legge, "perfect virtue" '.

★38. *A diseased notion of what constitutes 'sin'.* If we are to retain this term 'sin' at all, it is necessary to define it. Nothing can be properly called sinful unless it be (not only injurious in its outward effects but) a sin against the Light or Holy Ghost (the figure of speech does not matter) *in oneself*—a violation of one's deepest instincts. The one dogma of 'true religion and undefiled', as I understand it, is that the original impulse of the soul of man is towards love both of himself and of his kind, towards

[168]

The Liberation of Love

the (emotional not intellectual) recognition in others of that
vital spirit which he shares with all sentient things: this is 'the
love of God' translated into terms of humanism. It is to be
noted that love of self, deplorable only when it *ends* with self
(see Traherne, 84), is a necessary condition of the larger, out-
going love. Without self-respect, without self-love, without
honesty with himself, a man cannot respect, love, or be honest
with, others. The deepest and truest part of our knowledge of
others is derived from what we know of ourselves. Love, as cannot be too often repeated, is the only vital and positive impulse;
hate being an effect of love's frustration and perversion, deriving
the only life it can be said to have from the very thing of which
it seems to be (and, in effect, is) the contradiction. Hate is a
disguised manifestation of fear, and fear presupposes love, either
love of oneself alone, or that larger love in which self-love is
included and transcended. The liberation and wise expression
of love is thus seen to be the prime task of man's reason.

If my definition of 'sin' (with which this note opens) be
granted, it follows that sinfulness may often include many actions and abstentions commonly accounted virtuous; for precepts superstitiously received and rules blindly followed can
easily seduce us from fidelity to that deepest self, which is—to
borrow the language of mysticism—in some sense the Self of all
selves. We need, therefore, to be on our guard against false notions imposed on the mind by early training or by mere weight
of the general opinion—notions that are quite capable, not only
of assuming the guise of instinct, but even of masquerading, for
our confusion, as the Holy Ghost itself. The refusal of Jeanie

The 'Inner Light'

Deans to tell the trivial lie that would save her sister from being hanged (Scott's *Heart of Midlothian*) is a pretty example of what the Artificial Conscience does for us when, in idleness or stupidity or fear, we blasphemously set it upon the Throne of God in our hearts.

★53. WHATEVER may have been in the mind of their author, these prayers happen to be couched in terms that admit very readily of a humanist interpretation. They are—if we choose so to regard them—aspirations dramatized as petitions: poetical apostrophes to that nobler part of our common humanity which is called, variously, God, the Christ, the Inner Light, and so on. If for the sake of that definition which poetry demands we personify this Light, it is no wild flight of fancy, but a symbol of profound truth, to salute it as the 'author of peace and lover of concord, in knowledge of whom standeth our eternal life, whose service is perfect freedom'. With equal assurance may we look to it to 'defend us in all assaults of our enemies', since its unrestricted operation, in the hearts of us and our 'enemies' alike, would persuade us all into the paths of reason and lovingkindness. And it is noteworthy that this (the first of the two paragraphs) is a prayer definitely for peace, not a prayer for the victory of our arms.

Eternal life: 'Eternal' should not be regarded as synonymous with 'everlasting': it belongs to a different order of ideas. 'Everlasting' implies an infinite extension of time. But to the conception of 'the eternal', time is irrelevant; and 'eternal', as an adjective, signifies not endless duration but the (presumed) positive quality inherent in timelessness.

Holy desires. The word *holy* is merely the Middle English *hool* with the suffix *y* added, and so, like *hale* (to which it is closely related), it originally meant *whole:* that is, healthy. It has since become infected, by association, with the sense of 'sacredness', an idea rooted in the primitive superstition called taboo. Anything supposed to possess a mysterious (and possibly dangerous) power—whether it were a king, a god, the phenomena of birth and of death, or the sexual parts of the body—became a subject of taboo, and therefore 'sacred'. In the restoration to *holiness* of its original meaning, that of spiritual wholeness or health, a definite ethical philosophy is implied. I think it was a seventeenth-century Quaker who summed up his doctrine of conduct in the sentence: 'Never act unless you can act with your whole self'. There is nothing holier than the heart's native desire.

★60. THE translation is a blend of Tyndale and the Authorized Version, with one word ('anxious') from the Revised Version.

Where rust and moth corrupte not, nor theves breake through. Tyndale has: 'where neither rust nor mothes corrupte, and where theves neither break up, nor yet steale'. The A.V. has: 'where neither moth nor rust doth corrupt, and where thieves do not break through nor steal'. The version adopted is a variant on these.

Wycked. Tyndale. 'Wicked' (*vide* Skeat) was originally a past participle, with the sense 'rendered evil', from the obsolete adjective 'wikke'—evil. It is therefore a more illuminating word

[171]

than the A.V. 'evil', being more in harmony with the conception of an original impulsive good, or love. 'You are as prone to love as the sun is to shine', says Traherne. Wickedness is an aberration.

But seke ye rather the kingdom of God. Tyndale has: 'But rather seke ye fyrst the kingdom of heven'. The A.V. has: 'But seek ye first the kingdom of God'. What does 'the kingdom of God' mean? The same, surely, as the Tao of Lao-Tze, the Jên of Confucius, the 'charity' of Saint Paul, the 'Inner Light' of the Quakers—in yet other words, the vital impulse of love. See 3, 37, 71, and 78; and ★37, ★53, and ★71.

Rightwisnesse. Tyndale. The word 'righteous' is a corruption of 'rightwis'. 'Righteousness' is, therefore, 'right-wiseness' or intuitive 'knowledge of right', not mere conformity to external rules. That, in practice, this knowledge is too often obscured by fears, frustrations, and confusions (which alone are the source of hates, greeds, and cruelties) is evident enough. But submission to arbitrary 'authority', whether of creed or code, is perhaps equally dangerous to the life of the spirit.

★71. THE religion called Taoism claims Lao-Tze as its founder. Its doctrines, however, are curiously unlike anything taught by him. Taoism has provided itself generously with gods and devils, magic and mumbo-jumbo; and with these things the *Tao* of Lao-Tze has no connexion whatever. Authorities are unable to give us an exact English equivalent of *Tao*, a word that appears to mean, variously, a path, a method, a state of being. Perhaps the spontaneous way of living recommended by Jesus—the way of the flower—is the core of the idea. It seems to be generally agreed that Lao-Tze nowhere affirmed the existence of a Personal Creator.

Unprejudiced readers of the sayings attributed to Jesus of Nazareth will remark that Taoism is not the only religion that presents a distortion of the teachings of its reputed founder.

★93. THERE is perhaps more sweetness and light in Traherne than in any other Christian writer. The spirit of Puritanism, which seeks to identify pleasure with wickedness and compensates itself for its abstentions with spiritual pride, was abroad in the world long before the sixteenth century, when the name was first invented. To 'enjoy the world' was no part of the programme of the early Christians, if Gibbon is to be believed; and it would possibly have surprised them to know that 'the abominable corruption of men in despising it' was to be denounced, in a later age, by a priest of the church they had helped to found. 'The acquisition of knowledge, the exercise of our reason or fancy, and the cheerful flow of unguarded conversation', says Gibbon, 'may employ the leisure of a liberal mind. Such amusements, however, were rejected with abhorrence, or admitted with the utmost caution, by the severity of the fathers, who despised all knowledge that was not useful to salvation, and who considered all levity of discourse as a criminal abuse of the gift of speech. In our present state of existence the body is so inseparably connected with the soul, that it seems to be our interest to taste, with innocence and moderation, the enjoyments of which that faithful companion is susceptible. Very different was the reasoning

[173]

of our devout predecessors; vainly aspiring to imitate the perfection of angels, they disdained, or they affected to disdain,
every earthly and corporeal delight. Some of our senses indeed
are necessary for our preservation, others for our subsistence, and
others again for our information, and thus far it was impossible
to reject the use of them. The first sensation of pleasure was
marked as the first moment of their abuse. The unfeeling can-
didate for heaven was instructed, not only to resist the grosser
allurements of the taste or smell, but even to shut his ears against
the profane harmony of sounds, and to view with indifference
the most finished productions of human art. Gay apparel, magnificent houses, and elegant furniture, were supposed to unite
the double guilt of pride and of sensuality; a simple and morti-
fied appearance was more suitable to the Christian who was certain of his sins, and doubtful of his salvation. In their censures
of luxury, the fathers are extremely minute and circumstantial;
and among the various articles which excite their pious indignation, we may enumerate false hair, garments of any colour except
white, instruments of music, vases of gold or silver, downy pil-
lows (as Jacob reposed his head on a stone), white bread, foreign
wines, public salutations, the use of warm baths, and the practice of shaving the beard, which, according to the expression of
Tertullian, is a lie against our own faces, and an impious attempt to improve the works of the Creator. When Christianity
was introduced among the rich and the polite, the observation
of these singular laws was left, as it would be at present, to the
few who were ambitious of superior sanctity. But it is always
easy, as well as agreeable, for the inferior ranks of mankind to

The Sanctity of Discomfort

claim a merit from the contempt of that pomp and pleasure, which fortune has placed beyond their reach. The virtue of the primitive Christians, like that of the first Romans, was very frequently guarded by poverty and ignorance.' [*Decline and Fall of the Roman Empire*, Chapter XV.]

LIST OF AUTHORS

A NOTE ON THE TYPE IN WHICH THIS BOOK IS SET

The text of this book was set on the linotype in Baskerville. The punches for this face were cut under the supervision of George W. Jones, an eminent English printer. Linotype Baskerville is a facsimile cutting from type cast from the original matrices of a face designed by John Baskerville. The original face was the forerunner of the "modern" group of type faces. ¶ John Baskerville (1706-75), of Birmingham, England, a writing-master, with a special renown for cutting inscriptions in stone, began experimenting about 1750 with punch-cutting and making typographical material. It was not until 1757 that he published his first work, a Virgil in royal quarto, with great-primer letters. This was followed by his famous editions of Milton, the Bible, the Book of Common Prayer, and several Latin classic authors. His types, at first criticized as unnecessarily slender, delicate, and feminine, in time were recognized as both distinct and elegant, and both his types and his printing were greatly admired. Printers, however, preferred the stronger types of Caslon, and Baskerville before his death repented of having attempted the business of printing. For four years after his death his widow continued to conduct his business. She then sold all his punches and matrices to the Société Littéraire-typographique, which used some of the types for the sumptuous Kehl edition of Voltaire's works in seventy volumes. —